SOLICITORS' ACCOUNTS

Second edition

Tina McKee

Series editors: Amy Sixsmith and David Sixsmith

First published in 2022 by Fink Publishing Ltd
Second edition published in 2023

British Library Cataloguing in Publication Data
A catalogue record for this book is available from the British Library
ISBN: 9781914213809

This book is also available in various ebook formats.
Ebook ISBN: 9781914213816

Multiple-choice questions advisor: Mark Thomas
Cover and text design by BMLD (bmld.uk)
Production and typesetting by Westchester Publishing Services (UK)
Commissioning by R Taylor Publishing Services
Development editing by Peter Hooper and Sonya Barker
Editorial management by Llinos Edwards
Indexing by Terence Halliday

Fink Publishing Ltd
E-mail: hello@revise4law.co.uk
www.revise4law.co.uk

Contents

This book incorporates the updates to the SQE Assessment Specification published in April 2023 which came into force from 1 September 2023. Please note that, unless otherwise expressly stated, the law covered in this book applies in both England and Wales.

Contributors

THE AUTHOR

Tina McKee is a senior lecturer in law at Lancaster University where she leads on skills development and widening participation. She was previously course leader for Year 1 students on the undergraduate law courses at the University of Central Lancashire. She is also a senior fellow of the Higher Education Academy and was an institutional nominee for a National Teaching Fellowship in 2020. She has extensive experience of teaching both undergraduates and postgraduates, including over 20 years of teaching accounts to law students.

SERIES EDITORS

Amy Sixsmith is a senior lecturer in law and programme leader for LLB at the University of Sunderland, and a senior fellow of the Higher Education Academy.

David Sixsmith is assistant professor at Northumbria Law School, and a senior fellow of the Higher Education Academy.

Introduction to Revise SQE

Welcome to *Revise SQE*, a new series of revision guides designed to help you in your preparation for, and achievement in, the Solicitors Qualifying Examination 1 (SQE1) assessment. SQE1 is designed to assess what the Solicitors Regulation Authority (SRA) refer to as 'functioning legal knowledge' (FLK); this is the legal knowledge and competencies required of a newly qualified solicitor in England and Wales. The SRA has chosen single best answer multiple-choice questions (MCQs) to test this knowledge, and *Revise SQE* is here to help.

PREPARING YOURSELF FOR SQE

The SQE is the new route to qualification for aspiring solicitors introduced in September 2021 as one of the final stages towards qualification as a solicitor. The SQE consists of two parts:

SQE1
- **Functioning legal knowledge (FLK)**
- two x 180 MCQs
- closed book; assessed by two sittings, over 10 hours in total.

SQE2
- **Practical legal skills**
- 16 written and oral assessments
- assesses six practical legal skills, over 14 hours in total.

In addition to the above, any candidate will have to undertake two years' qualifying work experience. More information on the SQE assessments can be found on the SRA website; this revision guide series will focus on FLK and preparation for SQE1.

It is important to note that the SQE can be perceived to be a 'harder' set of assessments than the Legal Practice Course (LPC). The reason for this, explained by the SRA, is that the LPC is designed to prepare candidates for 'day one' of their training contract; the SQE, on the other hand, is designed to prepare candidates for 'day one' of being a newly qualified solicitor. Indeed, the SRA has chosen the SQE1 assessment to be 'closed book' (ie without permitting use of any materials) on the basis that a newly qualified solicitor would know all of the information tested, without having to refer to books or other sources.

With that in mind, and a different style of assessments in place, it is understandable that many readers may feel nervous or wary of the SQE. This is especially so given that this style of assessment is likely to be different from what readers will have experienced before. In this *Introduction* and revision guide series, we hope to alleviate some of those concerns with guidance on preparing for the SQE assessment, tips on how to approach single best answer MCQs and expertly written guides to aid in your revision.

What does SQE1 entail?

SQE1 consists of two assessments, containing 180 single best answer MCQs each (360 MCQs in total). The table below breaks down what is featured in each of these assessments.

Assessment	Contents of assessment ('functioning legal knowledge')
FLK assessment 1	• Business law and practice • Dispute resolution • Contract • Tort • The legal system (the legal system of England and Wales and sources of law, constitutional and administrative law and European Union law and legal services)
FLK assessment 2	• Property practice • Wills and the administration of estates • Solicitors accounts • Land law • Trusts • Criminal law and practice

Please be aware that in addition to the above, ethics and professional conduct will be examined pervasively across the two assessments (ie it could crop up anywhere).

Each substantive topic is allocated a percentage of the assessment paper (eg 'legal services' will form 12–16% of the FLK1 assessment) and is broken down further into 'core principles'. Candidates are advised to read the SQE1 Assessment Specification in full (available on the SRA website). We have also provided a *Revise SQE checklist* to help you in your preparation and revision for SQE1 (see below).

HOW DO I PREPARE FOR SQE1?

Given the vastly different nature of SQE1 compared to anything you may have done previously, it can be quite daunting to consider how you could possibly prepare for 360 single best answer MCQs, spanning 11 different substantive topics (especially given that it is 'closed book'). The *Revise SQE FAQ* below, however, will set you off on the right path to success.

Revise SQE FAQ

Question	Answer
1. Where do I start?	We would advise that you begin by reviewing the assessment specification for SQE1. You need to identify what subject matter can be assessed under each substantive topic. For each topic, you should honestly ask yourself whether you would be prepared to answer an MCQ on that topic in SQE1.
	We have helped you in this process by providing a *Revise SQE checklist* on our website (revise4law.co.uk) that allows you to read the subject matter of each topic and identify where you consider your knowledge to be at any given time. We have also helpfully cross-referenced each topic to a chapter and page of our *Revise SQE* revision guides.
2. Do I need to know legal authorities, such as case law?	In the majority of circumstances, candidates are not required to know or use legal authorities. This includes statutory provisions, case law or procedural rules. Of course, candidates will need to be aware of legal principles deriving from common law and statute.
	There may be occasions, however, where the assessment specification does identify a legal authority (such as *Rylands v Fletcher* in tort law). In this case, candidates will be required to know the name of that case, the principles of that case and how to apply that case to the facts of an MCQ. These circumstances are clearly highlighted in the assessment specification and candidates are advised to ensure they engage with those legal authorities in full.

Revise SQE FAQ (continued)

Question	Answer
3. Do I need to know the history behind a certain area of law?	While understanding the history and development of a certain area of law is beneficial, there is no requirement for you to know or prepare for any questions relating to the development of the law (eg in criminal law, candidates will not need to be aware of the development from objective to subjective recklessness). SQE1 will be testing a candidate's knowledge of the law as it stands four calendar months prior to the date of the first assessment in an assessment window.
4. Do I need to be aware of academic opinion or proposed reforms to the law?	Candidates preparing for SQE1 do not need to focus on critical evaluation of the law, or proposed reforms to the law either.
5. How do I prepare for single best answer MCQs?	See our separate *Revise SQE* guide on preparing for single best answer MCQs below.

Where does *Revise SQE* come into it?

The *Revise SQE* series of revision guides is designed to aid your revision and consolidate your understanding; the series is not designed to replace your substantive learning of the SQE1 topics. We hope that this series will provide clarity as to assessment focus, useful tips for sitting SQE1 and act as a general revision aid.

There are also materials on our website to help you prepare and revise for the SQE1, such as a *Revise SQE checklist*. This *checklist* is designed to help you identify which substantive topics you feel confident about heading into the exam – see below for an example.

Revise SQE checklist

Solicitors' Accounts

SQE content	Corresponding chapter	*Revise SQE checklist*		
Client money and client accounts • Definition and categories of client money	Chapter 2, Pages 17–19	I do not know this subject and I am not ready for SQE1 ☐	I partially know this subject, but I am not ready for SQE1 ☐	I know this subject and I am ready for SQE1 ☐

Solicitors' Accounts (continued)

SQE content	Corresponding chapter	Revise SQE checklist		
Client money and client accounts • Meaning and name of a client account	Chapter 2, Pages 19–21	I do not know this subject and I am not ready for SQE1 ☐	I partially know this subject, but I am not ready for SQE1 ☐	I know this subject and I am ready for SQE1 ☐
Client money and client accounts • Requirement to pay client money into a client account, including accounting entries	Chapter 2, Pages 21–26	I do not know this subject and I am not ready for SQE1 ☐	I partially know this subject, but I am not ready for SQE1 ☐	I know this subject and I am ready for SQE1 ☐
Client money and client accounts • Circumstances in which client money may be withheld from a client account	Chapter 2, Page 26	I do not know this subject and I am not ready for SQE1 ☐	I partially know this subject, but I am not ready for SQE1 ☐	I know this subject and I am ready for SQE1 ☐
Client money and client accounts • Requirements for client money held in a client account	Chapter 3, Pages 34–36	I do not know this subject and I am not ready for SQE1 ☐	I partially know this subject, but I am not ready for SQE1 ☐	I know this subject and I am ready for SQE1 ☐
Client money and client accounts • Requirements for withdrawals from a client account, including accounting entries	Chapter 3, Pages 36–41	I do not know this subject and I am not ready for SQE1 ☐	I partially know this subject, but I am not ready for SQE1 ☐	I know this subject and I am ready for SQE1 ☐
Client money and client accounts • Prohibition on using a client account to provide banking facilities	Chapter 3, Page 41	I do not know this subject and I am not ready for SQE1 ☐	I partially know this subject, but I am not ready for SQE1 ☐	I know this subject and I am ready for SQE1 ☐

Solicitors' Accounts (continued)

SQE content	Corresponding chapter	Revise SQE checklist		
Client money and client accounts • Requirement to keep client money separate from business money	Chapter 3, Pages 42–43	I do not know this subject and I am not ready for SQE1 ☐	I partially know this subject, but I am not ready for SQE1 ☐	I know this subject and I am ready for SQE1 ☐

PREPARING FOR SINGLE BEST ANSWER MCQs

As discussed above, SQE1 will be a challenging assessment for all candidates. This is partly due to the quantity of information a candidate must be aware of in two separate sittings. In addition, however, an extra complexity is added due to the nature of the assessment itself: MCQs.

The SRA has identified that MCQs are the most appropriate way to test a candidate's knowledge and understanding of fundamental legal principles. While this may be the case, it is likely that many candidates have little, if any, experience of MCQs as part of their previous study. Even if a candidate does have experience of MCQs, SQE1 will feature a special form of MCQs known as 'single best answer' questions.

What are single best answer MCQs and what do they look like?

Single best answer MCQs are a specialised form of question, used extensively in other fields such as in training medical professionals. The idea behind single best answer MCQs is that the multitude of options available to a candidate may each bear merit, sharing commonalities and correct statements of law or principle, but only one option is absolutely correct (in the sense that it is the 'best' answer). In this regard, single best answer MCQs are different from traditional MCQs. A traditional MCQ will feature answers that are implausible in the sense that the distractors are 'obviously wrong'. Indeed, distractors in a traditional MCQ are often very dissimilar, resulting in a candidate being able to spot answers that are clearly wrong with greater ease.

In a well-constructed single best answer MCQ, on the other hand, each option should look equally attractive given their similarities and subtle differences. The skill of the candidate will be identifying which, out of the options provided, is the single best answer. This requires a much greater level of engagement with the question than a traditional MCQ would require; candidates must take the time to read the questions carefully in the exam.

For SQE1, single best answer MCQs will be structured as follows:

A woman is charged with battery, having thrown a rock towards another person intending to scare them. The rock hits the person in the head, causing no injury. The woman claims that she never intended that the rock hit the person, but the prosecution allege that the woman was reckless as to whether the rock would hit the other person.

The factual scenario. First, the candidate will be provided with a factual scenario that sets the scene for the question to be asked.

Which of the following is the most accurate statement regarding the test for recklessness in relation to a battery?

A. There must have been a risk that force would be applied by the rock, and that the reasonable person would have foreseen that risk and unjustifiably taken it.

B. There must have been a risk that force would be applied by the rock, and that the woman should have foreseen that risk and unjustifiably taken it.

C. There must have been a risk that force would be applied by the rock, and that the woman must have foreseen that risk and unjustifiably taken it.

D. There must have been a risk that force would be applied by the rock, and that both the woman and the reasonable person should have foreseen that risk and unjustifiably taken it.

E. There must have been a risk that force would be applied by the rock, but there is no requirement that the risk be foreseen.

The question. Next, the candidate will be provided with the question (known as the 'stem') that they must find the single best answer to.

The possible answers. Finally, the candidate will be provided with **five** possible answers. There is only one single best answer that must be chosen. The other answers, known as 'distractors', are not the 'best' answer available.

Now that you know what the MCQs will look like on SQE1, let us talk about how you may go about tackling an MCQ.

How do I tackle single best answer MCQs?

No exact art exists in terms of answering single best answer MCQs; your success depends on your subject knowledge and understanding of how that subject knowledge can be applied. Despite this, there are tips and tricks that may be helpful for you to consider when confronted with a single best answer MCQ.

1. Read the question twice	2. Understand the question being asked	3. Select the answer if you know it outright	4. If not, employ a process of elimination	5. Take an educated and reasoned guess	6. Skip and come back to it later

1. Read the entire question at least twice

This sounds obvious but is so often overlooked. You are advised to read the entire question once, taking in all relevant pieces of information, understanding what the question is asking you and being aware of the options available. Once you have done that, read the entire question again and this time pay careful attention to the wording that is used.

- **In the factual scenario:** Does it use any words that stand out? Do any words used have legal bearing? What are you told and what are you not told?
- **In the stem:** What are you being asked? Are there certain words to look out for (eg 'should', 'must', 'will', 'shall')?
- **In the answers:** What are the differences between each option? Are they substantial differences or subtle differences? Do any differences turn on a word or a phrase?

You should be prepared to give each question at least two viewings to mitigate any misunderstandings or oversights.

2. Understand the question being asked

It is important first that you understand what the question is asking of you. The SRA has identified that the FLK assessments may consist of single best answer MCQs that, for example,

- require the candidate to simply identify a correct legal principle or rule
- require the candidate to not only identify the correct legal principle or rule, but also apply that principle or rule to the factual scenario
- provide the candidate with the correct legal principle or rule, but require the candidate to identify how it should be properly applied and/or the outcome of that proper application.

By first identifying what the question is seeking you to do, you can then understand what the creators of that question are seeking to test and how to approach the answers available.

3. Select the answer if you know it outright

You may feel as though a particular answer 'jumps out' at you, and that you are certain it is correct. It is very likely that the answer is correct. While you should be confident in your answers, do not allow your confidence (and perhaps overconfidence) to rush you into making a decision. Review all of your options one final time before you move on to the next question.

4. If you do not know the answer outright, employ a process of elimination

There may be situations in which the answer is not obvious from the outset. This may be due to the close similarities between different answers. Remember, it is the 'single best answer' that you are looking for. If you keep this in your mind, it will thereafter be easier to employ a process of elimination. Identify which answers you are sure are not correct (or not the 'best') and whittle down your options. Once you have only two options remaining, carefully scrutinise the wording used in both answers and look back to the question being asked. Identify what you consider to be the best answer, in light of that question. Review your answer and move on to the next question.

5. Take an educated and reasoned guess

There may be circumstances, quite commonly, in which you do not know the answer to the question. In this circumstance, you should try as hard as possible to eliminate any distractors that you are positive are incorrect and then take an educated and reasoned guess based on the options available.

6. Skip and come back to it later

If time permits, you may think it appropriate to skip a question that you are unsure of and return to it before the end of the assessment. If you do so, we would advise

- that you make a note of what question you have skipped (for ease of navigation later on), and
- ensure you leave sufficient time for you to go back to that question before the end of the assessment.

The same advice is applicable to any question that you have answered but for which you remain unsure.

We hope that this brief guide will assist you in your preparation towards, and engagement with, single best answer MCQs.

GUIDED TOUR

Each chapter contains a number of features to help you revise, apply and test your knowledge.

Make sure you know   Each chapter begins with an overview of the main topics covered and why you need to understand them for the purpose of the SQE1 assessments.

xiv   Introduction to Revise SQE

SQE assessment advice This identifies what you need to pay particular attention to in your revision as you work through the chapter.

What do you know already? These questions help you to assess which topics you feel confident with and which topics you may need to spend more time on (and where to find them in the chapter).

Key term Key terms are highlighted in bold where they first appear and defined in a separate box.

Exam warning This feature offers advice on where it is possible to go wrong in the assessments.

Revision tip Throughout the chapters are ideas to help you revise effectively and be best prepared for the assessment.

Summary This handy box brings together key information in an easy to revise and remember form.

Practice example These examples take a similar format to SQE-type questions and provide an opportunity to see how content might be applied to a scenario.

Procedural link Where relevant, this element shows how a concept might apply to another procedural topic in the series.

Key point checklist At the end of each chapter there is a bullet-point summary of its most important content.

Key terms and concepts These are listed at the end of each chapter to help ensure you know, or can revise, terms and concepts you will need to be familiar with for the assessments.

SQE-style questions Five SQE-style questions on the chapter topic give you an opportunity to test your knowledge.

Answers to questions Check how you did with answers to both the quick knowledge test from the start of the chapter and the SQE questions at the end of the chapter.

Key cases, rules, statutes and instruments These list the key sources candidates need to be familiar with for the SQE assessment.

SQE1 LEGAL AUTHORITIES

The SQE1 Assessment Specification states the following in respect of legal authorities and their relevance to SQE1:

> On occasion in legal practice a case name or statutory provision, for example, is the term normally used to describe a legal principle or an area of law, or a rule or procedural step (eg *Rylands v Fletcher*,

CPR Part 36, Section 25 notice). In such circumstances, candidates are required to know and be able to use such case names, statutory provisions etc. In all other circumstances candidates are not required to recall specific case names, or cite statutory or regulatory authorities.

You are not required to know any legal authorities for the purpose of the SQE1 Functioning Legal Knowledge assessments for *Solicitors' Accounts*.

TABLE OF STATUTES

Foundations of solicitors' accounts

■ MAKE SURE YOU KNOW

This chapter covers a great deal of the foundational information that will support you to answer SQE1 assessment questions correctly.

The SRA Accounts Rules 2019 (the Rules)

How the SQE1 Assessment Specification for Solicitors' Accounts maps onto the Rules

The dual system of accounting in law firms

- Business money and business bank accounts
- Client money and client bank accounts

Double-entry book-keeping

Layout of ledgers

- Ledgers with only business columns
- Ledgers with both business and client columns

Journal entries

■ SQE ASSESSMENT ADVICE

As you work through this chapter, remember to pay particular attention in your revision to:

- the Solicitors Regulation Authority (SRA) Accounts Rules 2019 and how they map onto the SQE1 Assessment Specification for Solicitors' Accounts
- why law firms and solicitors should comply with the SRA Accounts Rules 2019
- the definitions for *client money* and *business money*
- how law firms use the double-entry book-keeping system as the basis for their accounting records so that every financial transaction has a debit (DR) entry in one ledger and a balancing credit (CR) entry in a second ledger
- how law firms use a *dual system of accounting* to keep *client money separate from business money.*

■ WHAT DO YOU KNOW ALREADY?

Have a go at these questions before reading this chapter. If you find some difficult or you cannot remember the answers, make a note to look more closely at that during your revision.

1) What is the primary purpose of the SRA Accounts Rules?

   [The Rules, page 3]

2) What is double-entry book-keeping?

   [Double-entry book-keeping, page 7]

3) True or false? For every debit entry in a ledger, there must always be a corresponding credit entry in another ledger.

   [Double-entry book-keeping, page 7]

4) True or false? It does not matter whether client money is paid into either a business bank account or a client bank account.

   [Client money and client bank accounts, page 6]

5) Why do some ledgers, such as the cash sheet and client ledgers, have different columns for business transactions and client transactions?

   [Ledgers with both business and client columns, page 10]

INTRODUCTION

Some law students find solicitors' accounts intimidating because it involves numbers and accounting. Others find it easier because it seems to make sense naturally to them. Whatever your feelings about solicitors' accounts right now, I can assure you that investing time and effort in your revision will help you reach the standard required to answer the solicitors' accounts questions on the SQE1 assessment, that is, that of a competent newly qualified solicitor. In over 20 years of teaching solicitors' accounts, I have seen many students overcome their concerns so that they are able to answer accounts questions confidently and correctly.

However, remember that understanding solicitors' accounts is more than just about passing your SQE1 assessment. It is also vital for your future career in legal practice. You may already work in a law firm or be planning to work in one soon. You may also aspire to partnership or management roles within a firm. **The Rules** apply to everyone involved in a business that provides legal services, at whatever level, so you will need to know and comply with the Rules throughout your career. The consequences of non-compliance are serious, including criminal liability in some cases. The most recent Annual Report of the Solicitors' Disciplinary Tribunal (available on the Tribunal's website) reveals that 25% of all substantiated allegations of misconduct (both dishonest and accidental) arose from breaches of the Rules.

Key term: the Rules

Please note that all references to 'the Rules' throughout this book relate to **the SRA** Accounts Rules 2019. This version has been in effect since November 2019 and can be found on the SRA website. The Rules govern how law firms operate their accounting systems, and focus specifically on safeguarding money belonging to clients and others.

Key term: the SRA

The SRA is the Solicitors Regulation Authority, the professional regulator for the solicitors' branch of the legal profession which regulates how solicitors, law firms and other authorised bodies operate.

THE RULES

Law firms are businesses. Like all businesses, they must keep accounts that record all the financial transactions in which they are involved. For example, a law firm may buy new computing equipment or pay wages to its employees. These transactions must be recorded in the accounts of the business, sometimes called 'the books' of the business.

However, law firms are different from most businesses because many of their legal services require them to hold money belonging to their clients or on behalf of other third parties. For example, in a matter involving the administration of a deceased's estate, a **fee earner** will collect the assets of the person who has died before distributing them to the beneficiaries. Many of these assets will constitute money that is held in the firm's bank accounts while the fee earner undertakes the legal services required to complete the matter. However, this money *does not belong to the law firm*.

It is vital that *clients trust law firms to take good care of their money and to keep it safe*. Therefore, law firms must comply with stricter accounting rules than businesses that do not deal with money belonging to clients.

The SRA writes and publishes the strict rules that govern how law firms must run their accounts and, specifically, how they must look after client money (the Rules). The primary purpose of the Rules is to keep clients' money safe.

Key term: law firm(s) or firm(s)

All references in this book to 'law firm(s)' or 'firm(s)' encompass the definition of an 'authorised body', or 'licensed body' as defined in the Rules. In essence, these definitions include any bodies that are authorised or licensed by the SRA to offer legal services.

Key term: fee earner

A fee earner is a solicitor or other employee of a law firm who undertakes the legal work required in a particular matter. The fee earner charges the client for this legal work.

In addition to the Rules, the SRA publishes Principles and Codes of Conduct on its website. These include key points that will support your understanding of solicitors' accounts when preparing for the SQE1 assessment, as follows:

- Principle 2 – You act in a way that upholds *public trust and confidence* in the solicitors' profession.
- Principle 4 – You act with *honesty*.
- Code of Conduct for Solicitors Para 4.2 and Code of Conduct for Firms Para 5.2 – You *safeguard money* and assets *entrusted* to you by clients and others.

Again, these reinforce the SRA's focus on maintaining client trust and keeping money belonging to clients, and others, safe.

SQE1 ASSESSMENT SPECIFICATION FOR SOLICITORS' ACCOUNTS

Solicitors' accounts will be assessed as part of FLK (Foundation of Legal Knowledge) Assessment 2. Questions on solicitors' accounts may be set within the context of one, or a combination of several, of the other subject areas within FLK Assessment 2, that is, property practice; wills and administration of estates; land law; trusts; and criminal law and practice. The practice questions in this book reflect this breadth of context.

The SQE1 Legal Knowledge specification for solicitors' accounts reflects the Rules very closely. **Table 1.1** shows how the SQE1 specification maps onto the Rules and tells you where to find the content in this book. You are not required to know the numbers of the Rules for the SQE1 assessment. However, you will need to understand both the principles in the Rules as well as the *accounting entries* required for certain key transactions (*accounting entry* requirements are highlighted in italics in **Table 1.1**).

Table 1.1: How the SQE1 Assessment Specification for Solicitors' Accounts maps onto the Rules

SQE1 specification	The Rules	Chapter
Client money: • Definition • Requirement to pay client money into a client account	Rule 2	**Chapters 2 and 3**

Table 1.1: (continued)

SQE1 specification	The Rules	Chapter
• Circumstances in which client money may be withheld from a client account • Repayment • *Accounting entries required*		
Client account: • Meaning and name of account • Obligation not to use a client account to provide banking facilities • Withdrawals and *accounting entries required*	Rule 3 Rule 5	Chapters 2 and 3
Requirement to keep client money separate from money belonging to the authorised body	Rule 4	Chapter 2
Interest: • Requirement to pay interest on client money • *Accounting entries required*	Rule 7	Chapter 4
Breach of the SRA Accounts Rules: • Duty to correct breaches of SRA Accounts Rules promptly on discovery • *Accounting entries required*	Rule 6	Chapter 3
Requirement to keep and maintain accurate records in a client ledger, including requirement to carry out reconciliation of client accounts and to keep a record of bills to include: • Disbursements using the agency and principal methods • Transfers • Submission, reduction and payment of bills including the VAT element • *Accounting entries required*	Rule 8	Chapter 8 Chapter 6 Chapter 5 Chapters 5 and 6
Operation of joint account; operation of a client's own account	Rules 9 and 10	Chapter 7
Third-party managed accounts	Rule 11	Chapter 7
Obtaining and delivery of accountants' reports; storage and retention of accounting records	Rules 12 and 13	Chapter 8

THE DUAL SYSTEM OF ACCOUNTING IN LAW FIRMS

Law firms are different from most other types of business in that not only do they handle money that belongs to themselves, but also money that belongs to others, for example, their clients.

Rule 4.1 requires every firm to keep money that belongs to *clients* (or others) *separate* from money that belongs to *the firm*. Therefore, firms must use a dual system of accounting to ensure that it is clear from their accounting records which financial transactions relate to money that belongs to the firm, and which relate to money that belongs to others. Firms must also use *separate bank or building society accounts* to maintain this important separation of money.

Business money and business bank accounts

Most businesses use bank or building society accounts from which money is regularly paid in or out to keep the business running. These accounts may be instant access current accounts for daily use or deposit accounts for longer-term saving. All the money in the accounts belongs to the businesses themselves.

Payments out of the accounts may be to buy assets (eg business premises, fixtures and fittings, stationery, vehicles, etc); or to pay expenses of the business (eg wages, utility bills, rent, other overheads, etc). Payments into the accounts may be money received from selling goods or services.

Law firms are the same as any other business in that they also need bank accounts from which to buy assets or pay expenses, and into which they can pay the income received from selling legal services. In law firms, the money that belongs to the firm is called **business money** and any business money transactions will involve payments into, or out of, **business bank accounts**.

Key term: business money

Business money is money that belongs to the law firm rather than to its clients.

Key term: business bank account

A business bank account is one that is used by a law firm to receive, or make payments of, business money.

However, law firms are different from most businesses in that they often hold money belonging to their clients or others while providing legal services. The next section considers this in more detail.

Client money and client bank accounts

To provide legal services effectively, law firms must often hold or receive money that belongs to a *client or third party*. This money does not belong to the business so it cannot be paid into a business bank account. Instead, it is defined by the Rules as **client money** and any transactions relating to receipts or payments of client money must be into, or from, a **client bank account**. Firms usually have a *general client account* (see **Chapter 2, page 20** for the definition as a key term) in which money belonging to their clients and others is held. They may also have other client bank accounts, for example deposit accounts to hold money for specific clients where large sums may be held for longer periods of time (see **Chapter 4**).

Much of the rest of this book considers how firms must comply with the Rules to ensure that client money is kept safe.

Key term: client money

Client money is any money over which a solicitor or the firm has control, but which does not belong to the firm. Rule 2.1 defines *client money*. In essence, this includes money held or received by a law firm on behalf of clients or third parties when delivering legal services; money held or received which is intended to cover the firm's fees before a bill has been delivered, or expenses before they have been paid out (see **Chapter 5**); and money held or received by a solicitor while acting in specific roles (see **Chapter 7** for more details of these types of roles).

Key term: client bank account

A client bank account is one that is used by a law firm to receive, or make payments of, client money.

DOUBLE-ENTRY BOOK-KEEPING

Accounting records of businesses are based on a system called **double-entry book-keeping**. This system means that a business will make two entries in its **ledgers** for every financial transaction that occurs.

Key term: double-entry book-keeping

Double-entry book-keeping is a system used by businesses across the world to keep track of their financial transactions. For each transaction there is a debit and credit entry (the double-entry) in two different ledgers (the books). These entries balance each other out (balancing the books).

Key term: ledgers

A ledger is a record of financial transactions. In the old days, ledgers were kept in books and this is where the term 'book-keeping' came from originally. Most law firms now use online ledgers as part of their business accounting software. Different ledgers are used to record different aspects of the firm's financial transactions, for example cash sheets, assets ledgers, expenses ledgers, profit costs ledgers, creditors' ledgers, debtors' ledgers, capital ledgers, etc.

The two entries in the ledgers for any financial transaction are the 'double-entry' and they must be equal and opposite to each other. One entry is a *debit entry* (abbreviated to *DR*), which records something that may be seen as 'good' for the business; and the other entry will be a *credit entry* (abbreviated to *CR*) which records something that may be seen as 'bad' for the business.

> ## Revision tip
>
> Ledgers are drawn up from the perspective of the business, not the customer or client, so in simplistic terms:
> - Debit (DR) = good for the business.
> - Credit (CR) = bad for the business.
>
> This is opposite to what you are used to when looking at your own bank statements. You are a customer of the bank (the business), so your bank statement is simply a copy of your client ledger prepared by the bank from its own perspective. Therefore:
> - A *debit* balance or overdraft on your bank statement means that you owe the bank money (bad for you but *good for the bank*).
> - A *credit* balance on your bank statement means that the bank owes you money (good for you but *bad for the bank*).

Double-entry book-keeping ledgers form the basis for the profit and loss account and balance sheet that businesses, including law firms, use to give a summary of the financial status of their business at key points in time, for example at the end of the business's annual accounting period. (See *Revise SQE: Business Law and Practice* for more information.)

LAYOUT OF LEDGERS

This section will remind you about the different types of ledgers that a law firm may use. First, we will look at ledgers that just relate to business transactions, and then we will look at ledgers that record both business and client money transactions.

Ledgers with only business columns

Many ledgers record financial transactions relating to just the firm. These ledgers will just have three *business columns* as they only deal with transactions using *business money*. The entries in the business columns usually relate to money paid into or out of the firm's *business bank account(s)*, although they may also relate to other things such as *debts owed to the firm* (eg by clients with outstanding bills), or *liabilities owed by the firm* (eg creditors, such as software suppliers or suppliers of stationery, to whom money is owed by the firm, or lenders from whom the firm has taken out a loan).

Examples of such ledgers include:
- asset ledgers, for example for premises, fixtures and fittings, vehicles, computer software, etc

- expense ledgers, for example for wages, utility bills, fuel costs, buildings maintenance, etc
- **profit costs** ledger which records the legal work done by the firm's fee earners, for which clients have been billed.

Key term: profit costs

Profit costs are sometimes called professional fees or charges. The firm will charge the client profit costs for legal services provided.

An example of an extract from a profit costs ledger, showing the three business columns, is shown in **Figure 1.1**. There is a *debit (DR)* column, a *credit (CR)* column and a column showing the running total of the *balances* on the ledger. The entries represent the bills delivered to a range of clients in connection with the legal services provided by the firm.

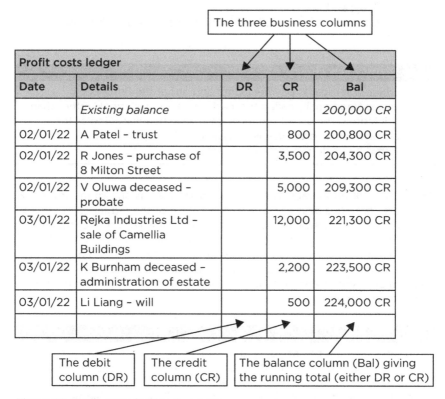

The three business columns		

Profit costs ledger					
Date	Details	DR	CR	Bal	
	Existing balance			*200,000 CR*	
02/01/22	A Patel – trust		800	200,800 CR	
02/01/22	R Jones – purchase of 8 Milton Street		3,500	204,300 CR	
02/01/22	V Oluwa deceased – probate		5,000	209,300 CR	
03/01/22	Rejka Industries Ltd – sale of Camellia Buildings		12,000	221,300 CR	
03/01/22	K Burnham deceased – administration of estate		2,200	223,500 CR	
03/01/22	Li Liang – will		500	224,000 CR	

The debit column (DR)	The credit column (CR)	The balance column (Bal) giving the running total (either DR or CR)

Figure 1.1: Profit costs ledger (extract)

Note: The double entries for each of the transactions in the profit costs ledger will be made in the client ledgers for each respective client as a debit (DR) entry in the business columns for profit costs (see **Chapter 5** for more details on ledger entries when billing clients).

Ledgers with both business and client columns

As most law firms hold money on behalf of clients and others (as well as money belonging to the firm), some of their ledgers must have three *client columns* as well as three *business columns*. Financial transactions relating to *business money* paid into or out of the firm's *business bank account(s)* will be recorded in the *business columns;* and transactions relating to *client money* paid into or out of the firm's *client account(s)* will be recorded in the *client columns*. Other transactions relating to either the firm or the client will also be recorded in the appropriate columns. Examples may include entries relating to profit costs and VAT in the *business columns* (see **Chapter 5, Submitting a bill**), and inter-client transfers in the *client columns* (see **Chapter 6, Inter-client transfers**).

Examples of ledgers with both business and client columns include:
• the **cash sheet** which records payments and receipts of both business and client money; and
• *client ledgers* that are specific to individual clients and their legal matters.

Key term: cash sheet

The ledger that records payments into and out of the firm's bank accounts is traditionally called the 'cash sheet' or 'cash book' rather than the cash ledger. The use of the term 'cash' may be misleading as the transactions do not often involve physical cash, but more usually money transferred by bank transfers or by cheque.

An example of an extract from a firm's cash sheet is shown in **Figure 1.2**. There are *three business columns* in the centre of the ledger (debit, credit and balance) and *three client columns* on the right-hand side of the ledger (debit, credit and balance). The entries represent payments or receipts of business money into and out of the business bank account, and payments or receipts of client money into and out of the client bank account. The entries relate to different clients and the different legal matters in which the firm is acting on their behalf.

Revision tip

The client account balance column on the far right of *the cash sheet* should always show a debit (DR) balance. A credit (CR) balance in the client account balance column on the cash ledger would indicate that the account is overdrawn, which is a breach of the Rules (see **Chapter 3** for more information on breaches of the Rules and how to correct them).

Cash sheet

Date	Details	Business account			Client account		
		DR	CR	Bal	DR	CR	Bal
	Existing balances			*450,500 DR*			*987,000 DR*
02/01/22	R Diaz purchase of 1 Brook Street – on account			450,500 DR	300		987,300 DR
02/01/22	N Noblett probate – payment of valuation fees		100	450,400 DR			987,300 DR
02/01/22	T Hussain sale of 8 Vale Street – HM Land Registry registration fees			450,400 DR		200	987,100 DR
03/01/22	D Okotete power of attorney – bill paid	300		450,700 DR			987,100 DR
03/01/22	G Randall administration of estate – payment of funeral expenses			450,700 DR		4,800	982,300 DR
03/01/22	E Rani sale of Darkling House – on account			450,700 DR	2,000		984,300 DR
04/02/22	Kaya Properties Ltd commercial lease – bill paid	5,000		455,700 DR			984,300 DR

Annotations:
- The three business columns
- The three client columns
- The debit columns (DR)
- The credit columns (CR)
- The balance columns (Bal) giving the running totals

Figure 1.2: Cash sheet (extract)

Note: The double entries for each of the transactions in the cash sheet will be made in a range of different ledgers, including client ledgers. For every debit entry on the cash sheet, a corresponding credit entry will be made on the second ledger, and for every credit entry on the cash sheet, a corresponding debit entry will be made on the second ledger.

Revision tip

Although you do not need to complete ledgers for the SQE1 assessment, some of the questions may test your knowledge of the *accounting entries* required in different situations. It is therefore essential to have a good understanding of how ledger entries are made. Many people find it easier to recall the correct ledger entries by visualising a ledger. This book will therefore give lots of examples of different ledgers to help you memorise what ledgers look like and how different accounting entries in these ledgers must be made to comply with both the principles of double-entry book-keeping and the Rules.

To prepare for SQE1 questions relating to *accounting entries*, your revision should focus on:
- In which *two ledgers* will the accounting entries be made?
- Does the transaction involve *business* or *client money*?
- Which ledger will have the *debit (DR)* entry, and which will have the *credit (CR)* entry?

JOURNAL ENTRIES

As the SQE1 assessment consists of single best answer multiple-choice questions, it is unlikely that you will see ledgers in either the questions or choice of answers. However, the SQE1 Assessment Specification indicates that you may be assessed on *accounting entries* for certain key financial transactions. It is likely that questions that test your understanding of accounting entries will present possible options in the form of **journal entries**. Therefore, you need to be familiar with how double-entry accounting transactions are summarised in this way.

Key term: journal entries

Journal entries are a *description* or *summary* of accounting entries made in a firm's ledgers. They are used as a quick way of explaining what double entries are required in which of the firm's ledgers for any financial transaction.

In keeping with the general principles of double-entry book-keeping discussed earlier in this chapter, you should expect journal entries to include both a debit (DR) entry and a corresponding credit (CR) entry that is equal and opposite to it. The journal entries should therefore identify:
- which *two ledgers* are involved in the transaction;
- whether the transaction relates to *client* or *business money* (entries will either both be in the client or both in the business account); and
- which entry is the *debit (DR)* and which is the *credit (CR)*.

The journal entries for different transactions can be *written* in different ways but the *content* of the double entries relating to the specific transaction that they represent will always be the same. See **Figure 1.3** for the information that you would expect journal entries to include, however they are written.

First ledger entry	Credit (or CR)	Name of the ledger in which the CR entry is made	Client account or business account (depending on whether the transaction relates to client money or business money)
Second ledger entry	Debit (or DR)	Name of the ledger in which the DR entry is made	Client account or business account (depending on whether the transaction relates to client money or business money)

There must always be one credit (CR) entry and one debit (DR) entry to balance the double entry for the transaction	You must decide which two ledgers the accounting entries should appear in for each type of transaction	You must decide whether the transaction relates to *client money* or *business money*. The double entries will either *both* be in the *client account* or *both* in the *business account* accordingly

Figure 1.3: Information included in journal entries to summarise a double-entry transaction

Exam warning

To identify the appropriate journal entries from a choice of answers on the SQE1 assessment, you will need to answer the same three questions highlighted in the revision tip in the previous section:

1) In which *two ledgers* should the double entries appear?
2) Does the transaction relate to *client money* or *business money*?
3) Which entry should be *debit (DR)*, and which should be *credit (CR)*?

Once you have answered these questions, you will be able to identify the correct journal entries from the choice of answers on the SQE1 assessment.

■ KEY POINT CHECKLIST

This chapter has covered the following key knowledge points. You can use these to structure your revision around, making sure to recall the key details for each point, as covered in this chapter.

- The Solicitors' Accounts specification for SQE1 maps closely onto the Rules, so you need to know how the Rules apply in practice contexts, and how certain accounting entries should be made in accordance with the Rules.
- Firms hold and receive money that belongs to clients and others (*client money*). They must comply with the Rules to keep client money safe, and to keep it separate from money belonging to the business (*business money*).
- Firms use a dual system of accounting (so that some of the ledgers have both business and client columns) so that it is clear whether transactions relate to *business* or *client money.*
- Firms must use different bank (or building society) accounts for *business money* and *client money.*
- Firms use the *double-entry book-keeping system,* that is, for every financial transaction, there will be a *debit (DR) entry in one ledger and a balancing credit (CR) entry* in a second ledger.
- SQE1 questions may assess your understanding of *accounting entries* by using *journal entries.*
- *Journal entries* for a transaction will identify the *two ledgers* involved, which ledger will contain the *credit (CR) entry* and which the *debit (DR) entry,* and whether the transaction relates to *business money* or *client money.*

■ KEY TERMS AND CONCEPTS

- the Rules (**page 3**)
- the SRA (**page 3**)
- law firm(s) or firm(s) (**page 3**)
- fee earner (**page 4**)
- business money (**page 6**)
- business bank account (**page 6**)
- client money (**page 7**)
- client bank account (**page 7**)
- double-entry book-keeping (**page 7**)
- ledgers (**page 7**)
- profit costs (**page 9**)
- cash sheet (**page 10**)
- journal entries (**page 12**)

■ SQE1-STYLE QUESTIONS

The other chapters in this book include five SQE1-style questions per chapter. However, as this chapter provides foundational information only, it is not appropriate to include any SQE1-style questions here.

■ ANSWERS TO QUESTIONS

Answers to 'What do you know already?' questions at the start of the chapter

1) The primary purpose of the Rules is to keep client money safe.
2) Double-entry book-keeping is a system for recording financial transactions. For each transaction there is a debit and credit entry (the double-entry) in two different ledgers (the books). These entries balance each other out (balancing the books).
3) True. The debit and credit entries for every transaction must always balance each other. They should either both appear in the business account columns of two different ledgers, or in the client account columns of two different ledgers.
4) False. Client money must *always* be paid into a client bank account. It is a breach of the Rules to pay it into a business bank account (unless it is a mixed receipt of both client money and business money paid initially into a business bank account, from which the client money element is promptly transferred to the client bank account – see **Chapter 6, Mixed receipts**).
5) Most law firms deal with client money and must therefore keep client money separate from business money to comply with the Rules, for example by using separate bank accounts for client and business money. Firm ledgers that record transactions relating to client money (eg the cash sheet or client ledgers) must have separate client columns to record such transactions.

■ KEY RULES

The SRA Accounts Rules 2019 can be found on the SRA website.

The SQE1 Assessment Specification for Solicitors' Accounts does not require you to know individual Rule numbers, just the principles underpinning the Rules. However, you should familiarise yourself with the operation of Rule 4.1 so that you can answer questions on the separation of *business money* and *client money.*

2

Client money and client accounts: part 1

■ MAKE SURE YOU KNOW

This chapter is structured around elements of the SQE1 Assessment Specification relating to client money and client accounts, including definitions of key terms, and requirements when paying client money into client accounts. It includes the following topics:

Client money

- Definition of client money

Client account

- Requirements for a client account
- Different types of client account
- Firms that do not use a client account

Client money and client accounts

- Requirement to pay client money into a client account promptly
- Accounting entries for a receipt of client money
- Example ledger entries for a receipt of client money
- Journal entries for a receipt of client money
- Circumstances in which client money may be withheld from a client account

■ SQE ASSESSMENT ADVICE

As you work through this chapter, remember to pay particular attention in your revision to:
- the definition of *client money* (Rule 2.1)
- how *client money* is different from *business money*
- the definition of a *client account*
- the requirements for where a client account may be held and how it should be named (Rules 3.1 and 3.2)
- the different types of client account that a firm may operate
- the circumstances in which some firms can choose not to operate a client account

- the general principle requiring that client money is paid promptly into a client account (Rule 2.3)
- the exceptions to this general principle, that is circumstances in which client money may be withheld from a client account (Rule 2.3(a)–(c))
- the *accounting entries* required to record a receipt of client money into a client account.

■ WHAT DO YOU KNOW ALREADY?

Have a go at these questions before reading this chapter. If you find some difficult or cannot remember the answers, make a note to look more closely at that during your revision.

1) What is the difference between business money and client money?
   [Client money, page 17]
2) True or false? All law firms must operate a client account.
   [Client account, page 19]
3) What is the general requirement for the timescale in which client money should be paid into a client account?
   a) immediately
   b) promptly
   c) within 14 days of receipt.
   [Client money and client accounts, page 21]
4) What are the double entries required for recording a receipt of client money?
   [Accounting entries for a receipt of client money, page 22]
5) True or false? Client money must always be paid into a client account.
   [Client money and client accounts, page 21]

CLIENT MONEY

As stated in **Chapter 1**, law firms often receive or hold money that does not belong to the firm. This money is usually held on behalf of clients or others while the firm provides legal services. The SRA Accounts Rules (the Rules – see **Chapter 1**) contain important requirements for solicitors and firms to make sure that this money is kept safe.

In this chapter we will consider *client money* and *client accounts* in more detail.

Client money is any money that a law firm receives or holds that does not belong to the firm. Money that belongs to the firm is *business money*. Rule 2.1 provides the definition of client money.

> ### Key term: client money
> There are four categories of client money defined in Rule 2.1. These can be summarised briefly as:
> 1) Money held on behalf of *clients* while providing them with legal services.

2) Money held on behalf of *third parties* while providing legal services to clients.
3) Money held by *solicitors acting in certain specified roles.*
4) Money held on *account of costs and unpaid disbursements prior to delivery of a bill.*

The four categories of client money are considered in more detail in the sections below.

Money held on behalf of clients

Rule 2.1(a) provides that client money includes money held on behalf of a *client*, relating to **regulated services** delivered to a *client*. In essence, this is money that is held on behalf of the client, whatever its source, during a legal matter. Examples include the net proceeds of sale in residential or commercial property transactions, or monies collected in administering a deceased's estate.

Key term: regulated services

Regulated services are defined in the Rules as the legal and other professional services that firms are regulated by the SRA to provide. The definition includes a solicitor acting as a trustee or as the holder of a specified appointment. For the purposes of this book, regulated services will be referred to as *legal services* for ease of understanding.

Money held on behalf of third parties

Rule 2.1(b) provides that client money includes money held on behalf of a *third party* in relation to *regulated services* delivered by the solicitor or firm. In essence, this is money held on behalf of the *third party* rather than the *client.* For example, in a property sale transaction, a solicitor may receive a deposit from the buyer that is held either as *agent* (ie on behalf of the buyer) or as *stakeholder* (ie on behalf of the buyer as well as the seller) until the sale is completed (see **Chapter 7, Stakeholder deposits** and **Deposits held as agent** for more details). It also includes money *held to the sender's order* (ie where a third party sends money to the solicitor to be held on their behalf until they confirm it can be released to the client, or they request that the solicitor returns it to them).

Money held by solicitors acting in certain specified roles

Rule 2.1(c) provides that client money includes money held by a solicitor acting in a certain specified role. Such roles include acting as a *trustee* for a trust, a *donee of a power of attorney*, a *Court of Protection deputy*, or a *trustee* of an occupational pension scheme (see **Chapter 7, Client's own account** for definitions of a 'donee of a power of attorney' and a 'Court of Protection deputy'). In any of these roles, a solicitor may find themselves responsible for money that does not belong to the firm, and as such, they must ensure that they comply with the Rules in keeping such client money safe, together with any additional requirements associated with the specified role that they hold.

Money held on account of costs and unpaid disbursements prior to delivery of a bill

Rule 2.1(d) provides that client money includes money held in respect of **fees** and any unpaid **disbursements** held or received prior to delivery of a bill. Essentially, if a client sends money *on account of the firm's fees and disbursements*, such money is treated as client money until a bill is delivered. See **Chapter 5** for more details on fees and **Chapter 6** for more details on disbursements and VAT.

Key term: fees

Fees are defined in the Rules as the firm's own charges or profit costs (including any VAT element). In essence, this means the fees charged to clients for the legal services provided to them by the firm.

Key term: disbursements

Disbursements are defined in the Rules as 'any costs or expenses paid or to be paid to a third party on behalf of the client or trust (including any VAT element) save for office expenses such as postage and courier fees'. Essentially, this means that any fees or expenses paid to third parties with respect to the legal matter involved are deemed to be disbursements (apart from those that are part of the firm's general expenses associated with providing legal services). For example, counsel's fees, conveyancing search fees and Land Registry registration fees are all disbursements.

CLIENT ACCOUNT

In the next section we will consider the general rule that *client money* should be held in a *client account*, and any exceptions to that rule. However, first we will look at the meaning of a client account, that is what a **client account** actually is.

Key term: client account

A client account is a bank or building society account in which a firm holds *client money.*

Requirements for a client account

Most firms operate client accounts. Under Rule 3.1, all client accounts must be held at either a bank or building society in England or Wales. This is to protect client money by ensuring that it is kept in an institution authorised to provide banking facilities, and by preventing it from being transferred to another country.

Rule 3.2 requires that any client account must be labelled with both:
- the name of the firm; and
- the word 'client'.

This is so that *client money* held in a *client account* is clearly distinguishable from any *business money* held in a firm's *business account* (in accordance with the Rule 4.1 requirement that *client money must be kept separate from business money* – see **Chapter 1**). This is important because, for example, if a firm were to be subject to any insolvency proceedings, only *business money* should be used to pay off any debts owed to the firm's creditors. *Client money* held in a clearly labelled *client account* cannot be touched by the insolvency practitioners as it is obvious from the name of the account that the money belongs to clients or other third parties, rather than to the firm.

Different types of client account

In general, firms operate a **general client account** into which they pay most of the client money that they hold for clients and other third parties. Payments will be made from the general client account to progress the legal matters in which the firm is acting on behalf of its clients.

Key term: general client account

A general client account is the main *client account* operated by most firms. It is a bank or building society account which holds *client money* from lots of different clients and other third parties. The balance on a firm's general client account is therefore usually high. It is important that firms have robust record keeping so that they can identify which portion of client money belongs to which individual client at any point in time. Therefore, individual client ledgers must be maintained for individual clients with respect to the legal matters in which the firm is acting for them. See **Chapter 1** for more details on client ledgers and **Chapter 8** for more details on firms' obligations for accounting records.

However, in some instances, firms may pay client money into separate client accounts relating to individual client matters. This may be appropriate where a legal matter requires that a firm holds a significant sum of money for a protracted period. These accounts may be called *separate designated deposit client accounts* or something similar. See **Chapter 4** for more details on these types of client accounts.

Firms that do not operate client accounts

A small minority of firms do not operate any client accounts. This may be because a firm has chosen to use a third-party business, separate to the firm, to manage the firm's client money in *third-party managed accounts*. See **Chapter 7** for more information on such accounts.

Alternatively, under Rule 2.2 there is also an exception whereby a firm does not need to have a client account in which to hold client money if:
* the only client money that the firm receives is money received in respect of their own fees and any unpaid disbursements (this only includes disbursements that the firm is liable to pay, for example counsel's fees) prior to delivery of a bill (see **Chapter 5** for details on delivering bills);
* the firm does not operate a client account for any other purpose; and
* the firm has told clients in advance where and how the money will be held.

This is quite a limited exception which will not apply to firms undertaking most areas of legal practice. However, a firm that purely offers criminal litigation services may benefit from the exception. For example, if the only client money received by the firm is payment for their fees and disbursements from the Legal Aid Agency (LAA), this money can be paid into the firm's *business account* and there is no need for the firm to have a *client account* at all (see **page 26** for further information on dealing with payments from the LAA).

Some of the other Rules do not apply to client money where the firm does not have a client account. For example, the firm is not required to keep client money separate from business money, or client money does not have to be available on demand.

CLIENT MONEY AND CLIENT ACCOUNTS

In this section we will explore the general principle that client money must be paid into a client account, together with any exceptions to this principle, and the associated Rules. We will also consider the accounting entries that are used when client money is paid into the client account.

Requirement to pay client money into a client account promptly

The general principle set out in Rule 2.3 is that all client money is paid *promptly* into a client account. Although there is no definition of 'promptly' in the Rules, it is expected that client money received by bank transfer should either be sent directly to the client account or transferred into the client account very shortly afterwards (see **Chapter 6** for more details on transfers following mixed receipts of both client money and business money). For client money received in cash or by cheque, it seems reasonable to expect it to be paid into the client bank account on the same, or the next, working day.

Practice example 2.1 demonstrates how Rule 2.3 should be applied in practice.

Practice example 2.1

A solicitor is acting for the personal representatives of a deceased woman in the administration of her estate. One of the personal representatives brings in £15 cash that he found in a biscuit tin in the deceased woman's home. The solicitor is in a rush so puts the money in her desk drawer and then forgets about it until three weeks later.

Has the solicitor breached the Rules and what action should she take next?

The solicitor has not acted correctly as the £15 cash is client money that should have been paid into the client account promptly when received. The solicitor and firm are therefore in breach of the Rules and must correct this breach promptly by taking the £15 cash to the bank and paying it into the client bank account immediately (see Chapter 3 for more details on how to correct breaches of the Rules).

Accounting entries for a receipt of client money

We have considered the general principle that client money is paid promptly into a client account once received. In addition to understanding this principle, you also need to know the *accounting entries* required to record such receipts of client money.

Client money will be received from clients and third parties in many different types of legal matters. For example, in a probate matter, the firm may receive money from different sources as the deceased's assets are collected in, before distribution to the beneficiaries. This might include money received on the closure of the deceased's bank accounts, the receipt of a life insurance payment, or the net proceeds of sale from the deceased's home, etc.

For each receipt of client money, a double entry must be made using the firm's cash sheet and the individual client ledger. Both entries will be in the client account columns and the credit (CR) entry will be in the client ledger, while the debit (DR) entry will be in the cash sheet (see **Chapter 1** for more details on the principles of double-entry book-keeping).

Example ledger entries for a receipt of client money

The following example demonstrates how receipts of client money in a particular legal matter are recorded in the client ledger and cash sheet.

A solicitor is instructed by the personal representatives of Sajid Al Aziz, recently deceased, in the administration of his estate. The solicitor receives the following sums of client money early in the period of administration:
• 6th January – £300 from the personal representatives on account of costs and disbursements.

- 15th January – £1,025 cash found in Sajid's safe in his home.
- 20th January – £55,000 received from Sajid's life insurance.

It does not matter whether the receipts are in cash, by cheque or by bank transfer, they must all be paid into the client bank account and recorded as credits on the client ledger and debits on the cash sheet. **Figure 2.1** shows how the client ledger and cash sheet would look in this scenario.

Client ledger: Personal representatives of Sajid Al Aziz deceased (extract) Matter: Administration of estate							
		Business account			Client account		
Date	Details	DR	CR	Bal	DR	CR	Bal
6/1	Cash – on account					300	300 CR
15/1	Cash – money from safe					1,025	1,325 CR
20/1	Cash – life insurance					55,000	56,325 CR

Cash sheet (extract)							
		Business account			Client account		
Date	Details	DR	CR	Bal	DR	CR	Bal
	Existing balances			XX			XX DR
6/1	S Al Aziz deceased – from PRs on account			XX	300		XX DR
15/1	S Al Aziz deceased – money from safe in home			XX	1,025		XX DR
20/1	S Al Aziz deceased – life insurance received			XX	55,000		XX DR

Figure 2.1: Ledger entries for receipts of client money

Journal entries for a receipt of client money

In **Chapter 1**, we considered how the SQE1 assessment might test your understanding of accounting entries by asking you to identify the correct journal entries for a transaction from a range of options.

To identify the correct journal entries for a *receipt of client money* you must answer the key questions as shown in **Table 2.1**.

Table 2.1: Questions to help identify the correct journal entries for a receipt of client money

1. In which two ledgers should the double entries appear?	The client ledger and the cash sheet
2. Does the transaction relate to client money or business money?	Client money so the client account must be used
3. Which entry should be debit (DR) and which should be credit (CR)?	CR on the client ledger and DR on the cash sheet

The journal entries for a *receipt of client money* will always include the information identified in **Table 2.1**, although the correct option in an SQE1 assessment may appear in any of the following ways:
• CR client ledger client account; and DR cash sheet client account.
• CR client ledger (client account); and DR cash sheet (client account).
• Credit client ledger client account; and debit cash sheet client account.
• Credit client ledger (client account); and debit cash sheet (client account).

Revision tip
You should memorise the journal entries for key financial transactions included on the SQE1 specification, for example for a receipt of client money. This will help you to identify the correct answers in the SQE1 assessment. This book will highlight which journal entries you need to revise as they arise in the relevant chapters.

As many journal entries will relate to either the client ledger or the cash sheet (or both), **Table 2.2** is a good starting point for your revision on accounting entries.

Table 2.2: Debits and credits to memorise for money going in and out of the client ledger and cash sheet

Ledger	Money in / out	CR or DR	Commentary
Client ledger	Money in	CR	Easy to remember on a client ledger as it is the *same on your own bank statement*
	Money out	DR	

Table 2.2: (continued)

Ledger	Money in / out	CR or DR	Commentary
Cash sheet	Money in	DR	Remember that credits and debits on a cash sheet are *opposite to your own bank statement*
	Money out	CR	

Practice example 2.2 demonstrates how accounting entries for receipts of client money may be assessed in the SQE1 assessment.

Practice example 2.2

A solicitor acts for a commercial property client in the sale of a leisure complex. On completion, the solicitor receives £10,000,000 from the buyers, representing the proceeds of sale.

What accounting entries are required to record the receipt of the proceeds of sale?

The proceeds of sale are *client money* that must be paid promptly into the *client account* in accordance with the Rules. The journal entries reflecting the double entries in the firm's ledgers are *CR client ledger client account £10,000,000; and DR cash sheet client account £10,000,000*.

Exam warning

Here are some top tips for answering SQE1 assessment questions on *accounting entries*:
1) *Read the question carefully* at least twice so that you know exactly what it is asking you to do.
2) *Decide what you think the correct double entry is* before looking at any of the answers to see if you can find one that matches.
3) *Read all the answer options carefully* at least twice. It is easy to misread answers (for example, don't mix up 'client ledger' and 'client account').
4) Check the answers to find ones that relate to the *correct two ledgers* (for example, client ledger and cash sheet for a receipt of client money).
5) Check the answers to make sure that the *double entries are either both in the client account or both in the business account*. You can eliminate any answers where one entry is in the client account and one is in the business account as this will not be a valid double entry.
6) Check the answers to make sure that there is *a debit (DR) entry that corresponds with a credit (CR) entry*. You can eliminate any answers with two debit entries or two credit entries as these will not be valid double entries.

7) *Check that the debit (DR) and credit (CR) entries are the right way around.* It is easy to muddle this, so memorise the entries for key transactions. You can also use certain key principles to help you revise this – see **Table 2.2.**

Circumstances in which client money may be withheld from a client account

Although the general principle is that client money should be paid into a client account promptly, there are three exceptions to this principle set out in Rule 2.3(a)–(c):

1) The first exception (in Rule 2.3(a)) relates purely to the category of client money defined in Rule 2.1(c), that is money that is held or received by a solicitor as a trustee or as the holder of a specified office or appointment (see **Chapter 7** for examples of such roles). This exception allows solicitors acting in these roles to comply with other role-specific requirements that may conflict with the general principle to pay client money promptly into a client account. For example, a Court of Protection appointed deputy will usually hold money belonging to an incapacitated person in a separate deputyship account.

2) The second exception (in Rule 2.3(b)) relates to payments from the **Legal Aid Agency (LAA)** for the firm's **costs.** For example, if the LAA pays for all the legal fees and disbursements involved in defending a criminal client, this will constitute the only client money handled by the firm while acting for the client. As such, the exception allows the money from the LAA to be paid straight into the firm's business account, even before a bill has been delivered (see **Chapter 5** for more details on delivering bills).

3) The third exception (in Rule 2.3(c)) provides that firms can agree alternative arrangements for holding client money with clients or third parties, providing the agreement is in advance and is recorded in writing. If such an agreement is in place, the firm can, for example, hold client money in a third-party managed account (see **Chapter 7** for more details).

Key term: Legal Aid Agency (LAA)

The Legal Aid Agency is a government body that funds solicitors and barristers to provide free legal advice, and sometimes legal representation, for clients who are eligible to receive it. LAA funding is available for both civil and criminal cases.

Key term: costs

Costs are defined in the Rules as both *fees* and *disbursements* (defined on **page 19**).

■ KEY POINT CHECKLIST

This chapter has covered the following key knowledge points. You can use these to structure your revision, making sure to recall the key details for each point, as covered in this chapter.

- There are four different categories of client money. They are money held on behalf of *clients*, money held on behalf of *third parties*, money held by *solicitors holding certain specified roles*, and *money on account of costs and unpaid disbursements*.
- A client account should be in a bank or building society in England or Wales. It should be named with the firm's name and include the word 'client'.
- Most, but not all, firms will operate client accounts. There are different types of client accounts including general client accounts (holding money on behalf of multiple clients and third parties) and separate designated deposit client accounts (holding money on behalf of a single client).
- The general principle is that client money should be paid into a client account promptly on receipt. However, there are certain exceptions to this principle.
- The accounting/journal entries for a receipt of client money are CR client ledger client account and DR cash sheet client account.

■ KEY TERMS AND CONCEPTS

- client money (**page 17**)
- regulated services (**page 18**)
- fees (**page 19**)
- disbursements (**page 19**)
- client account (**page 19**)
- general client account (**page 20**)
- Legal Aid Agency (LAA) (**page 26**)
- costs (**page 26**)

■ SQE1-STYLE QUESTIONS

QUESTION 1

A solicitor is in the process of setting up her own law firm. She plans to specialise in criminal defence work, funded by the Legal Aid Agency (LAA), and she will employ an associate solicitor to supervise a team of paralegals providing residential conveyancing services.

Will the firm need to operate a client account?

A. The firm must operate a client account because this is a standard requirement for all law firms regulated by the Solicitors Regulation Authority (SRA).

B. The firm does not need to operate a client account because it is specialising in criminal litigation defence work, funded by the LAA.

C. The firm should operate a client account unless it makes use of a third-party managed account instead.

D. The firm does not need to operate a client account because any client money received on account of professional fees and disbursements can be paid into the firm's business account.

E. The firm must operate a client account because all firms that offer criminal defence services are required to do so by the SRA.

QUESTION 2

A solicitor has been appointed as a deputy by the Court of Protection to look after the finances of a middle-aged man with learning difficulties, who lacks the mental capacity to manage his own affairs. The man's mother has recently died, leaving her whole estate to him in her will. The solicitor needs to decide what to do with any money that the man inherits as part of the estate.

Is the money for the man's inheritance deemed to be client money and should the solicitor pay it into the firm's general client account?

A. The money for the man's inheritance is deemed to be client money and therefore it must be paid into the firm's general client account.

B. The money for the man's inheritance is deemed to be client money but there is an exception in the Rules that does not require the solicitor to pay it into the firm's general client account.

C. The money for the man's inheritance is deemed to be client money and must be paid into a third-party managed account.

D. The money for the man's inheritance is not client money so it can be paid into the business account.

E. The money for the man's inheritance is not client money so the solicitor can pay it into a separate account on behalf of the man.

QUESTION 3

A solicitor is acting in a probate matter. They receive a payment of £150,000 from a life insurance company which had insured the life of the deceased.

What are the accounting entries required to record the receipt of the £150,000 life insurance payment?

A. £150,000 credit (CR) entry in client ledger client account and £150,000 debit (DR) entry in cash sheet client account.

B. £150,000 CR entry in client ledger client account and £150,000 CR entry in cash sheet client account.

C. £150,000 DR entry in client ledger client account and £150,000 CR entry in cash sheet client account.

D. £150,000 DR entry in client ledger business account and £150,000 CR entry in cash sheet client account.

E. £150,000 CR entry in client ledger client account and £150,000 DR entry in cash sheet business account.

QUESTION 4

A solicitor receives a cheque for £400 from a client on account of costs and disbursements in a residential conveyancing matter. The solicitor locks the cheque in her office drawer for safekeeping as the firm's cashier is not available to take the cheque to the bank. The solicitor then forgets about the cheque and goes on holiday for two weeks. While she is away, she recalls that the cheque is still locked in her office drawer, but that nobody else can access it as she has taken the only set of keys with her on holiday.

What action should the solicitor and her firm take with respect to the £400 cheque from the client?

A. There is no need for the solicitor or her firm to do anything until she returns from holiday, at which point the cheque can be paid into the client account at the bank.

B. As the cheque is on account of costs and disbursements, it consists of money that belongs to the firm. As such, there is no requirement for it to be paid into the bank until it is convenient for the solicitor to do so.

C. As the cheque consists of client money, the firm is in breach of the Rules as it has not been paid into the client account promptly. The firm should transfer £400 from the firm's business account into the client account temporarily until the cheque can be paid into the client account on the solicitor's return from holiday.

D. As the cheque is on account of costs and disbursements, there is no need for it to be paid into a bank account until after the firm has delivered a bill to the client.

E. The solicitor should return from holiday early so that she can unlock the drawer and ensure that the cheque is paid into the client account promptly.

QUESTION 5

Three solicitors decide to leave their current firm to set up a new law firm in partnership. They intend to specialise in commercial property.

What are the requirements for setting up the new firm's client account at the bank?

A. The firm should not operate a client account as they are unlikely to be holding client money as part of the legal services that they intend to offer.

B. The partners must all be signatories on the client account, which should be set up at a bank or building society located as close to the firm's new offices as possible.

C. The client account can be set up in any financial organisation in Great Britain that is regulated by the Financial Conduct Authority.

D. The client account must be set up in a bank or building society in England or Wales. The name of the account must include the name of the firm and be labelled as a client account.

E. The client account must be set up in a bank or building society in England or Wales. The name of the account must include the name of all the partners of the firm.

■ ANSWERS TO QUESTIONS

Answers to 'What do you know already?' questions at the start of the chapter

1) Business money is money that belongs to the firm whereas client money is money that is held by the firm on behalf of clients or third parties. Client money is held by the firm so that it can provide legal services to its clients effectively.

2) False. In some situations, firms will choose not to operate a client account. For example, a firm may choose to use a third-party managed account (see **Chapter 7** for more details on third-party managed accounts) or, providing certain criteria are met, a firm may not operate a client account where the only client money it receives is on account of its own professional fees and disbursements.

3) The correct answer was (b). The general requirement is that client money should be paid into a client account *promptly*.

4) The correct double entries for a receipt of client money are:
    • credit (CR) client ledger client account; and
    • debit (DR) cash sheet client account.

    The credit entry must be in the client ledger in the client account columns (this is like when you pay money into your own bank account and see a credit entry on your bank statement). The corresponding double entry must be a debit entry in the client account columns of the cash sheet.

5) False. There are some exceptions to the general principle that client
    money must be paid into a client account. See **Circumstances in which
    client money may be withheld from a client account, page 26,** for more
    details of these exceptions.

Answers to end-of-chapter SQE1-style questions

Question 1:
    The correct answer was C. This is because although most firms will have
    their own client account, they can *choose to use a third-party managed
    account* instead. Options A and E are incorrect because the Rules do not
    provide a blanket requirement for all firms (option A), or all firms offering
    criminal defence services (option E), to operate client accounts. One of the
    exceptions to the requirement for a client account is for firms where the
    only source of client money is the Legal Aid Agency on account of the firm's
    professional fees and disbursements. This does not apply in this case as the
    firm also offers conveyancing services and will hold client money associated
    with this area of work. Options B and D are therefore incorrect.

Question 2:
    The correct answer was B. This is because the definition of client money
    includes money held by a solicitor in certain specified roles, including
    as a deputy appointed by the Court of Protection (options D and E
    are therefore incorrect). However, client money in this category falls
    under one of the exceptions in the Rules to the general principle that
    client money must be paid into a client account (option A is therefore
    incorrect). Option C is incorrect as the Rules do not require client money
    in this category to be paid into a third-party managed account. It is
    advisable for the solicitor to pay the man's inheritance money into a
    separate deputyship account.

Question 3:
    The correct answer was A. The accounting entries for a receipt of client
    money are *CR client ledger and DR cash sheet.* Both entries must be
    in the *client account columns* to reflect the fact that the life insurance
    payment is client (rather than business) money. Option B is incorrect
    because it has two credit entries and therefore is not a valid double
    entry. Option C is incorrect because the credit and debit are the wrong
    way around. Options D and E are both incorrect because they mention
    the business account rather than the client account. Further, option D is
    incorrect because the credit and debit are also the wrong way around.
    Watch out for answers that do not include a debit and credit, or that mix
    up client account and business account, as these will not be valid double
    entries and can be eliminated as possible choices when deciding which
    answer is most likely to be correct.

Question 4:
    The correct answer was C. As the cheque is on account of costs and
    disbursements it meets the definition of *client money* in the Rules. It

should therefore have been *paid into the client account promptly*. The solicitor and her firm are therefore in breach of the Rules. To correct this breach, business money should be transferred immediately into the client account until the solicitor's return from holiday, when the cheque can be paid into the client account, and the corresponding money returned to the business account. Option E would also produce a correct remedy to the breach in the Rules, but there is no need for the solicitor to return from holiday when there is a faster but less drastic option (option C). Option A is incorrect because it allows a known breach of the Rules to continue rather than correcting it immediately on discovery. Option B is incorrect because the cheque consists of client money rather than business money. Option D is incorrect because client money on account of costs and disbursements should be paid into the client account promptly rather than waiting for a bill to be delivered, at which point it would become business money and could be transferred into the business account. See **Chapter 3** for more details on correcting breaches of the Rules.

Question 5:

The correct answer was D. This is because the Rules require a client account to be held in a bank or building society (rather than any financial organisation regulated by the Financial Conduct Authority as stated in option C). The location of the bank or building society must be in *England or Wales* (rather than in Great Britain as stated in option C). There is also no requirement for the account to be held near to the firm's offices (as stated in option B). The Rules require the account name to include the *name of the firm* and the word *'client'* so that the money in the account can be easily identifiable as *client money* simply from the account's name. There is no requirement for all partners to be signatories (option B) or for all partners' names to be on the account (option E). Option A is incorrect as the firm is likely to be holding large amounts of client money due to the nature of the commercial property legal services that they intend to offer.

■ KEY RULES

The SRA Accounts Rules 2019 can be found on the SRA website.

The SQE1 Assessment Specification for Solicitors' Accounts does not require you to know individual Rule numbers, just the principles underpinning the Rules. However, you should familiarise yourself with the operation of:

• Rule 2.1
• Rule 2.2
• Rule 2.3
• Rule 3.1
• Rule 3.2

3

Client money and client accounts: part 2

■ MAKE SURE YOU KNOW

This chapter is structured around elements of the SQE1 Assessment Specification relating to client money and client accounts, including withdrawals from client accounts and how to correct breaches of the SRA Accounts Rules ('the Rules' – see **Chapter 1**). It includes the following topics:

> Requirements for client money in a client account

> Client money available on demand

> Client money to be returned promptly

> Withdrawals from a client account
> - Accounting entries for withdrawals from a client account
> - Example ledger entries for withdrawals from a client account

> Prohibition on using a client account to provide banking facilities

> Requirement to keep client money separate from business money

> Breach of Accounts Rules
> - Duty to correct breaches promptly on discovery
> - Accounting entries to correct breaches

■ SQE ASSESSMENT ADVICE

As you work through this chapter, remember to pay particular attention in your revision to:
- ensuring that client money is *available on demand* unless there is an alternative written agreement between the firm and the client (Rule 2.4)
- *repaying client money promptly* when there is no longer any proper reason for holding it (Rule 2.5)
- understanding the situations in which client money can be *withdrawn* from a client account (Rule 5.1)

- requirements for appropriate *authorisation and supervision of withdrawals* from a client account (Rule 5.2)
- ensuring that client money is only withdrawn if *sufficient funds are held* on behalf of the specific client (Rule 5.3)
- the *accounting entries* required to record a *withdrawal* of client money from a client account
- the obligation *not to provide banking facilities* to clients (Rule 3.3)
- the requirement to keep *client money separate from business money* (money belonging to the authorised body) (Rule 4.1)
- the duty to *correct breaches* of the Rules *promptly upon discovery* (Rule 6.1)
- the *accounting entries* required to *correct a breach* of the Rules.

■ WHAT DO YOU KNOW ALREADY?

Have a go at these questions before reading this chapter. If you find some difficult or cannot remember the answers, make a note to look more closely at that topic during your revision.

1) True or false? Client money must always be available on demand.

   [Client money available on demand, page 34]

2) At the end of a legal matter, what is the requirement for returning client money to the relevant client or third party?

   [Client money to be returned promptly, page 35]

3) What important prohibition is contained in Rule 3.3?

   [Prohibition on using a client account to provide banking facilities, page 41]

4) True or false? Money sent by a client to cover a disbursement that has already been paid by the firm must be paid into the client account immediately.

   [Requirement to keep client money separate from business money, page 42]

5) What are the double entries for a withdrawal from the client account?

   [Accounting entries for withdrawals from the client account, page 38]

REQUIREMENTS FOR CLIENT MONEY IN A CLIENT ACCOUNT

Having considered how client money must be paid into (or withheld from) the client account in **Chapter 2**, this chapter will explore the Rules and requirements for *client money that is already in the client account*, including the requirements for *withdrawing client money*.

CLIENT MONEY AVAILABLE ON DEMAND

Rule 2.4 sets out the general principle that client money should be *available on demand* (ie immediately). This Rule acknowledges that client money does not belong to the firm, so the clients (or others for whom the money is held) can request it back at any time. In essence, this requires firms to maintain a general client account which is either a current account or a deposit account that requires no notice period for withdrawals.

However, Rule 2.4 also provides an exception to this general principle whereby a firm can agree with the client (or third party for whom money is held) that client money is *not available on demand*. Any such agreement must be in writing. For example, if a legal matter requires a firm to hold a large sum for a specific client over a significant period of time, the firm and client may agree that the money is held in a *separate designated deposit client account* (a separate client account where money is held on deposit for just one client) where a better rate of interest is available than for money held in the general client account. Separate designated deposit client accounts often require notice periods for withdrawal, so the money is no longer available on demand. However, the higher rates of interest may be more attractive for the client. See **Chapter 4** for more details on separate designated deposit client accounts and interest.

Practice example 3.1 indicates how this principle might be tested in the SQE1 assessment.

Practice example 3.1

A solicitor is acting for a client in the purchase of a residential property. The client sends £20,000 towards the deposit, which is paid into the firm's general client account. However, shortly before the deposit is due to be paid to the seller's solicitors, the client requests that the solicitor returns the £20,000.

What action should the solicitor take with respect to the £20,000?

The solicitor should return the £20,000 to the client in accordance with their request. It is client money, so should be available on demand. The solicitor cannot pay the money to the seller's solicitors as this is not in accordance with the client's most recent instructions and she cannot retain the money in the general client account.

CLIENT MONEY TO BE RETURNED PROMPTLY

Rule 2.5 sets out the general principle that a firm cannot hold client money indefinitely and that it must be returned to the client (or third party for whom it is held) as soon as there is no longer any proper reason for holding it. This means that once a legal matter has been completed, client money must be sent to the relevant party *promptly*. Although the Rules do not contain a definition of 'promptly', it is suggested that client money should be returned as quickly as possible when it is no longer needed for the provision of legal services. For example, at the end of a conveyancing transaction, any net proceeds of sale must be paid to the client as soon after completion as possible. In a probate matter, once all the legal work has been concluded and the estate accounts have been approved, the firm should distribute the deceased's assets to the beneficiaries promptly.

In some situations, it may be more difficult for a firm to know when to return client money. For example, a client may stop giving instructions when a legal matter is incomplete, and the firm is still holding client money on their behalf. This may be due to illness, accident or the client moving away. If the firm is unable to contact the client for further instructions to progress the matter, then the client money should be returned to the client, for example, by bank transfer to the client's bank account from which it was originally sent. If the firm cannot locate the client and does not know where to return the money, they should not keep the money. After a reasonable lapse of time and reasonable efforts to contact the client, the firm can seek approval from the SRA to withdraw the balance of client money and pay it to charity. No SRA approval is needed if the sum is less than £500.

Rule 2.5 may also link to Rule 3.3 which prohibits firms from providing banking services to clients (see **page 41**). If firms do not return client money promptly when there is no longer a proper purpose for holding it, they may also be at risk of providing banking facilities to their clients inadvertently. See **Chapter 4** for more examples relating to these Rules.

WITHDRAWALS FROM THE CLIENT ACCOUNT

Rule 5 regulates withdrawals of client money from the client account. Under Rule 5.1 there are three reasons why such withdrawals can be made:

1) Client money can be withdrawn for the purpose for which it is being held. This is the most common reason for withdrawals. For example, a client has paid a sum of money *on account of fees and disbursements* in a commercial property transaction. The firm can withdraw money from this sum in the client account to pay for disbursements such as survey fees or search fees. The firm can also transfer money to cover its own professional fees (profit costs) following delivery of an interim or final bill. See **Chapter 5** for more information on transfer of profit costs from the client account to the business account.

2) Client money can be withdrawn following instructions from the client or third party for whom it is held. **Practice example 3.1** illustrates this principle.

3) Following authorisation from the SRA. This may be necessary if a client cannot be located to give instructions while their money is still held in the client account (as discussed in the previous section).

However, all withdrawals from the client account must be carefully considered to ensure that client money is *kept safe* throughout the withdrawal process and that any withdrawal complies with the Rules. Therefore, Rule 5.2 requires firms to use robust procedures to authorise and supervise all withdrawals made from the client account. This means that the **managers** and **Compliance Officer for Finance and Administration (COFA)** for the firm must ensure that only people with sufficient seniority and understanding of the Rules are allowed to authorise withdrawals from the client account. They are also responsible for establishing systems and processes to *minimise any risks to client money* in the withdrawal process. For example, a firm's compliance policy may require a trainee solicitor to seek authorisation from a partner for any withdrawal from the client account.

Key term: manager

A manager of a firm is someone who has responsibility for running it. This could be:

- a partner in a law partnership;
- a member of a law LLP;
- the sole principal in a sole practice;
- a director of a law company.

Managers of law firms have joint and several responsibilities to ensure that their firm complies with the Rules (see Rule 1.2).

Key term: Compliance Officer for Finance and Administration (COFA)

All firms must have a COFA. The primary role of the COFA is to ensure that the firm complies with the Rules. The COFA does not have to be legally qualified, although many COFAs are. The COFA should set up and monitor systems within the firm to minimise any risks to client money and to ensure that all the firm's staff are trained to know how to comply with the Rules.

Rule 5.3 contains a very important requirement that *client money is only withdrawn if sufficient funds are held on behalf of that specific client or third party*, that is, that only the client money belonging to a specific client is withdrawn in order to progress that client's legal matter. As most client money is held in the firm's general client account, it is vital to know which portion of the money belongs to which client. If client A does not have sufficient client money in the general client account to progress their legal matter, the firm cannot use client B's money instead without breaching Rule 5.3. It is therefore essential that client ledgers for each client and matter are always up to date and accurate (see **Chapter 8** for requirements for record keeping with respect to client ledgers). A solicitor must check that there is a sufficient credit balance in the client account columns of the client's ledger before making any withdrawals to progress that client's legal matter.

Practice example 3.2 illustrates how your understanding of this issue might be tested in the SQE1 assessment.

Practice example 3.2

A solicitor is instructed by a client in a privately funded criminal defence case. The client sends the solicitor a cheque for £5,000 on account of fees and disbursements. The next day the solicitor makes a payment of £2,000 to a forensic specialist for preparation of her report. Unfortunately, the solicitor discovers later that day that the client's cheque has bounced, meaning that there was insufficient client money from which to pay the specialist.

What are the implications of the client's cheque bouncing after the forensic specialist has been paid?

The client's cheque bounces, which means that there is insufficient money in the general client account belonging to the client from which to pay the forensic specialist. Therefore, money belonging to other clients has been used instead, in breach of the Rules. To correct this breach, money must be transferred from the business account to the client account immediately. Once the client has provided sufficient funds to cover the specialist's invoice, the money can be transferred back into the business account.

To avoid this breach of the Rules, the solicitor should have waited until the client's cheque had cleared before paying the specialist's invoice. See page 43 for more details on breaches of the Rules and how to correct them.

Accounting entries for withdrawals from the client account

For the SQE1 assessment, you are expected to know what the accounting entries are for a withdrawal from the client account. Money may be withdrawn from the client account either:

1) to make a payment to the client or third party (this will be considered in more detail below); or
2) to make a transfer from client account to business account (see **Chapter 6** for more details on transfers from client account to business account).

Money may be withdrawn from the client account to send to the client. For example, at the end of a conveyancing sale transaction, the net proceeds of sale will be sent to the client following completion. Alternatively, money may be withdrawn from the client account to send to a third party. For example, at the end of a probate matter, the firm will distribute the remainder of the estate to the relevant beneficiary or beneficiaries. Monies may also be withdrawn from the client account to pay disbursements in an ongoing matter. For example, in a conveyancing transaction, payments may be made from the client account for disbursements such as search fees, Land Registry registration fees and Stamp Duty Land Tax.

In **Chapter 2**, we considered how to identify the correct journal entries for a receipt of client money. In this chapter, we will use the same three questions but in the context of a withdrawal from the client account (see **Table 3.1**).

Table 3.1: Questions to help identify the correct journal entries for a withdrawal of client money

1. In which two ledgers should the double entries appear?	The client ledger and the cash sheet
2. Does the transaction relate to client money or business money?	Client money so the client account must be used
3. Which entry should be debit (DR) and which should be credit (CR)?	DR on the client ledger and CR on the cash sheet

In an SQE1 assessment question, the correct journal entries for a *withdrawal from client account* may therefore be presented as *DR client ledger client account and CR cash sheet client account.*

Revision tip

Remember that the entries on the client ledger are similar to your own bank account, so when money is withdrawn there is a debit (DR) entry on the client ledger. The corresponding double entry on the cash sheet must therefore be opposite, that is, a credit (CR) entry.

Example of ledger entries for withdrawals from the client account

We will now continue the case study introduced in **Chapter 2** concerning the administration of the estate of Sajid Al Aziz deceased. Here, we will focus on the accounting entries in the client ledger and cash sheet for withdrawals from the client account.

As Sajid died intestate, without a surviving spouse or partner, the remainder of his estate must be shared equally between his three adult children, Laila, Jamilah and Faisal, in compliance with the Intestacy Rules. (See *Revise SQE: Wills and the Administration of Estates* for more information on the operation of the Intestacy Rules.) Each of these payments is a withdrawal from the client account, and the double entries must be recorded in both the client ledger and the cash sheet. All entries will be in the client account columns. **Figure 3.1** shows how the client ledger and cash sheet would look in this scenario.

Client ledger: Personal representatives of Sajid Al Aziz deceased (extract) Matter: Administration of estate							
		Business account			Client account		
Date	Details	DR	CR	Bal	DR	CR	Bal
	Existing balances			–			175,569 CR
5 Mar	Cash – payment to residuary beneficiary Laila Al Aziz			–	58,523		117,046 CR
5 Mar	Cash – payment to residuary beneficiary Jamilah Al Aziz			–	58,523		58,523 CR
5 Mar	Cash – payment to residuary beneficiary Faisal Al Aziz			–	58,523		–
5 Mar	Close ledger						

Cash sheet (extract)							
		Business account			Client account		
Date	Details	DR	CR	Bal	DR	CR	Bal
	Existing balances			XX			XX DR
5 Mar	S Al Aziz deceased – payment to residuary beneficiary Laila Al Aziz			XX		58,523	XX DR
5 Mar	S Al Aziz deceased – payment to residuary beneficiary Jamilah Al Aziz			XX		58,523	XX DR
5 Mar	S Al Aziz deceased – payment to residuary beneficiary Faisal Al Aziz			XX		58,523	XX DR

Figure 3.1: Ledger entries for withdrawals from the client account

Revision tip

For withdrawals (money paid out) from the client account, the accounting entries will be:

- money out = DR on *client ledger* client account (the *same* as on your own bank statement);
- money out = CR on *cash sheet* client account (the *opposite* to your own bank statement).

PROHIBITION ON USING A CLIENT ACCOUNT TO PROVIDE BANKING FACILITIES

Rule 3.3 is very important because it prohibits firms from using client accounts to provide banking facilities to their clients or other third parties.

Law firms are *not regulated* by the SRA to provide banking facilities. They are only regulated by the SRA to provide legal services to clients. As such, any *client money* held by them must be held for a purpose that is *directly related to this provision of legal services*. Firms must be very careful to refuse any instructions concerning client money that do not progress a legal matter in which they are acting. Breach of this Rule may increase the risk of involvement in money laundering, so the firm's managers and COFA should monitor compliance carefully to prevent this. See **Practice example 3.3** for how this topic may appear in the SQE1 assessment.

Practice example 3.3

A solicitor is instructed by a commercial property company in the sale of commercial retail buildings. On completion, the net proceeds of sale are paid into the firm's general client account. The same company has recently signed a lease for office premises in the business quarter of the city. The company instructs the solicitor to retain the proceeds of sale and to make monthly rental payments from the retained monies for the new offices.

What action should the solicitor take?

The solicitor must refuse the instructions to make rental payments on behalf of the company, as to do so would be to offer banking facilities. The rental payments are not associated with any legal matter in which the firm is acting and so the firm is not regulated to offer this service. Instead, the solicitor should return the net proceeds of sale to the company promptly so that the company can make its own rental payments.

For more examples relating to Rule 3.3, see **Chapter 4**.

REQUIREMENT TO KEEP CLIENT MONEY SEPARATE FROM BUSINESS MONEY

Rule 4.1 provides one of the fundamental principles underpinning the dual system of accounting used by law firms – that *client money should be kept separate from business money*. Therefore, most firms operate client accounts in which they hold client money separately from the firm's own business money, which is held in a business account (see **Chapter 2** for reasons why a minority of firms choose not to operate client accounts). This allows firms to identify balances of client money accurately at any time so that they can ensure it is kept safe in accordance with the Rules. Therefore, it is essential for firms to identify client money and business money when receiving or making payments.

Receipts of client money or business money

Receipts of client money are normally paid straight into the client account and receipts of business money are normally paid straight into the business account. Use **Table 3.2** to help you identify which receipts are client money and which are business money, and to remind you of the associated accounting entries. You should memorise these transactions and accounting entries for the SQE1 assessment.

Table 3.2: Receipts of business and client money, and associated accounting entries

Examples of receipts of money	
Business money to be paid into business account	*Client money* to be paid into *client account*
Money received in payment for *costs and disbursements following delivery of a bill* Money received for *paid disbursements, even before delivery of a bill* (providing this is the purpose for which the money is sent)	Money held on behalf of a *client* relating to legal services – Rule 2.1(a), eg proceeds of sale from a conveyancing transaction Money held on behalf of a *third party* relating to legal services provided to a client – Rule 2.1(b), eg a mortgage advance Money held by a solicitor in a *specified role* – Rule 2.1(c), eg as trustee Money received *on account of fees and unpaid disbursements prior to delivery of a bill* – Rule 2.1(d)

Table 3.2: (continued)

Accounting entries required	
Accounting entries for a receipt of *business money*	**Accounting entries for a receipt of** *client money*
• CR client ledger *business account* • DR cash sheet *business account*	• CR client ledger *client account* • DR cash sheet *client account*

For mixed receipts, which include elements of both client money and business money, see **Chapter 6** for more details.

Payments of client money or business money

Payments of client money should be made from the client account, and payments of business money should be made from the business account. Use **Table 3.3** to help you identify which payments are client money or business money, and to remind you of the associated accounting entries. You should memorise these transactions and accounting entries for the SQE1 assessment.

Table 3.3: Payments of business and client money, and associated accounting entries

Examples of payments of money	
***Business money* to be paid from** *business account*	***Client money* to be paid from** *client account*
Payments of disbursements using the *principal method* (see **Chapter 6**)	Payments relating to legal services, eg transfer of completion monies in a property purchase; or payment of gifts, legacies and residue to beneficiaries in a probate matter Payments of disbursements using the *agency method* (see **Chapter 6**)
Accounting entries required	
Accounting entries for a payment of *business money*	**Accounting entries for a payment** of *client money*
• DR client ledger *business account* • CR cash sheet *business account*	• DR client ledger *client account* • CR cash sheet *client account*

DUTY TO CORRECT BREACHES UPON DISCOVERY

Rule 6.1 is very important as it places a duty on firms and solicitors to correct any breaches of the Rules.

In **Chapter 2** and this chapter we have considered how the Rules regulate payments into and withdrawals from a client account. However, sometimes the Rules are breached where client money is not paid into a client account properly, or where money is withdrawn from a client account incorrectly. Here, we will focus on how to correct any such breaches.

The general principle in Rule 6.1 is that *any breaches of the Rules must be corrected promptly upon discovery.* There is no definition of 'promptly' in the Rules so firms should consider the type and context of the breach and consider how quickly the SRA would consider it reasonable for a firm to correct it. However, if the breach relates to money that has been improperly withheld or withdrawn from a client account, the breach must be remedied *immediately* by paying in or replacing the money in the client account.

Exam warning

If a question on the SQE1 assessment indicates that *any of the Rules have been breached*, look for an answer that indicates that the breach will be *corrected promptly on discovery*. If the question relates to money improperly withheld or withdrawn from a client account, the correct answer will state that such money must be *immediately* paid into or replaced in the client account (sometimes this will require a transfer from the business bank account to the client bank account).

The following sections include some examples of how to correct breaches of the Rules relating to payments in and out of a client account. However, you should be aware that there are many other ways in which the Rules might be breached and the same principle of correcting the breach promptly on discovery should be applied.

Accounting entries – client money paid into business account wrongly

If a receipt of client money is wrongly paid into the business account, Rule 2.3 will be breached (duty to ensure client money is paid promptly into a client account). To correct such a breach, the client money must be transferred from the business bank account into the client bank account *immediately* once the error is discovered. The journal entries required are:

1) To transfer the money out of the business account – DR client ledger business account and CR cash sheet business account.
2) To transfer the money into the client account – CR client ledger client account and DR cash sheet client account.

This is an example of a cash transfer (see **Chapter 6** for more details on cash transfers, including example ledgers).

This is illustrated in **Practice example 3.4**.

Practice example 3.4

A solicitor takes instructions from a new client in a conveyancing matter. She asks the client for £400 on account of costs and disbursements at the beginning of the matter and receives a cheque from the client for this amount. The solicitor pays the cheque into the firm's business bank account. This is in breach of the Rules as the solicitor has not yet delivered a bill to the client.

How should the solicitor correct this breach of the Rules?

The £400 is client money as the client has not yet received a bill. It should therefore have been paid into the client account on receipt. The solicitor should correct the breach of the Rules immediately by transferring £400 from the business bank account to the client bank account. The journal entries required to record this transfer are:

1) **DR £400 client ledger business account and CR £400 cash sheet business account (to transfer the client money out of the business bank account).**
2) **CR £400 client ledger client account and DR £400 cash sheet client account (to transfer the client money into the client bank account).**

Accounting entries – incorrect withdrawal of client money

Sometimes a breach of the Rules occurs when a withdrawal is made from the client account for a client who does not have sufficient funds to cover withdrawals for such a purpose. For example, a conveyancing client (client A) might be waiting for a mortgage advance from a lender to complete the purchase of a property. If the solicitor completes the purchase before the mortgage advance has been received, they have used money belonging to other clients held in the general client account, rather than the money belonging to client A. This is a breach of Rule 5.3 (duty to only withdraw client money from a client account if sufficient funds are held on behalf of that specific client to make the payment). Alternatively, a solicitor might breach Rule 5.1(a) by withdrawing client money from a client account for the right client but for the wrong purpose (for example, using a mortgage advance to pay for search fees).

Whenever such a breach occurs, the solicitor must correct the breach by immediately replacing the money in the client account. In practice, this may require the solicitor to transfer money from the business bank account to the client bank account to correct the breach. This is illustrated in **Practice example 3.5**.

Practice example 3.5

A solicitor is acting for a client (X) in a property sale and related purchase. The solicitors acting for the buyer (Y) have confirmed that the completion monies have been sent. On this basis, X's solicitor goes ahead and completes the related purchase, withdrawing money from the general client account to do so. Unfortunately, Y's solicitors then warn him that there has been an unexpected delay in the transfer of the completion monies from the sale transaction. On checking the general client bank account, the solicitor can see that the sale monies have not yet been received although the purchase monies have been withdrawn.

How should the solicitor respond to this situation?

This is a breach of Rule 5.3 because the money used to buy the purchase property does not belong to client X, as the sale monies from his house have not yet been received. This means that money belonging to other clients in the general client account has been used instead. In accordance with Rule 6.1, the solicitor must correct the breach upon discovery by immediately replacing the money that has been improperly withdrawn from the general client account. He should transfer the money from the firm's business bank account to the general client account temporarily until the completion monies from Y's solicitors have been received, at which point they can be transferred back into the business bank account.

■ KEY POINT CHECKLIST

This chapter has covered the following key knowledge points. You can use these to structure your revision around, making sure to recall the key details for each point, as covered in this chapter.

* Client money must be *available on demand* unless there is an alternative written agreement between the firm and the client.
* Client money must be returned to the client promptly when there is no longer any proper purpose for holding it.
* Client money can be withdrawn from the client account:
    1) for the purposes for which it is being held;
    2) following instructions from the client (or relevant third party for whom it is being held);
    3) following SRA authorisation.
* Client money must only be withdrawn if sufficient funds are held on behalf of the specific client.
* The *accounting entries* to record a withdrawal of client money from client account are:
    - DR client ledger client account; and
    - CR cash sheet client account.
* Firms are *prohibited from using a client account to provide banking facilities*, so money should be returned to clients promptly and firms should not take instructions to receive or pay out client money that are unrelated to the legal services that they provide to clients.
* *Client money* must always be *kept separate* from *business money*.

- The *accounting entries* for the following key transactions are:
  - Receipt of business money: CR client ledger business account and DR cash sheet business account.
  - Receipt of client money: CR client ledger client account and DR cash sheet client account.
  - Payment of business money: DR client ledger business account and CR cash sheet business account.
  - Payment of client money: DR client ledger client account and CR cash sheet client account.
- There is a duty for solicitors and firms to *correct breaches of the Rules promptly on discovery.* If the breach relates to client money improperly withheld or withdrawn from a client account, the breach must be corrected *immediately* by replacing the client money in the client account. This may involve transferring business money from the business account into the client account in some circumstances.

■ KEY TERMS AND CONCEPTS

- manager **(page 37)**
- Compliance Officer for Finance and Administration (COFA) **(page 37)**

■ SQE1-STYLE QUESTIONS

QUESTION 1

A solicitor is acting in a criminal defence case for a privately funded client. The solicitor has already paid the defence counsel's fee invoice from the business account as there were insufficient funds available in the client account. The solicitor has not yet delivered a bill to the client but has asked the client by telephone to send payment to cover the counsel's fees. The client sends a cheque for the relevant amount.

What should the solicitor do with this cheque?

A. The solicitor should deliver a bill to the client immediately so that the cheque can be paid into the firm's business account.

B. The solicitor should place the cheque in the client's file until a bill has been delivered, at which point, it can be paid into the firm's business account.

C. The solicitor should pay the cheque into the firm's business account as it is a receipt of business money.

D. The solicitor should pay the cheque into the firm's client account promptly as it is a receipt of client money.

E. The solicitor should pay the cheque into the firm's business account
    immediately as it is a receipt of client money.

QUESTION 2

A solicitor acts for a conveyancing client who is selling their old home and
purchasing a new one. Completion is due to take place on the same day for
both the sale and purchase. The solicitor receives an undertaking from the
buyer's solicitor that the proceeds from the sale will be transferred to the
firm's general client account by 3 P.M. on the completion date. Based on this
undertaking, the solicitor authorises the transfer of the completion monies
for the client's purchase matter. At the end of the day, the solicitor realises
that the proceeds of sale from the sale matter have not been received.

**What does the client ledger for the purchase matter show on the completion
date, and what action should the solicitor now take?**

A. The client ledger for the purchase shows a debit balance in the client
    account for this matter, in breach of the Rules. To correct this breach, the
    solicitor should transfer sufficient business money into the client account
    temporarily until the proceeds from the sale property are received.
B. The client ledger for the purchase will show a credit balance in the client
    account for this matter so there is no breach of the Rules. Accordingly,
    there is no need for the solicitor to do anything.
C. The client ledger for the purchase will show a debit balance in the
    business account for this matter. The solicitor should transfer sufficient
    funds from the client account into the business account to clear this
    debit balance.
D. The client ledger for the purchase will show a zero balance in both the
    client account and the business account. Accordingly, there is no need
    for the solicitor to do anything.
E. The client ledger for the purchase will show a debit balance in the client
    account. The solicitor should transfer sufficient funds from the sale
    matter to the purchase matter to clear this debit balance.

QUESTION 3

A solicitor is instructed by a commercial property client in the sale of an
office block. Following completion, the solicitor sends the net proceeds of
sale of £1,650,000 to the client.

**What accounting entries are required to record the transfer of the net
proceeds of sale to the client?**

A. Credit (CR) £1,650,000 cash sheet business account and debit (DR)
    £1,650,000 profit costs ledger.

B. DR £1,650,000 cash sheet client account and CR £1,650,000 client ledger client account.

C. DR £1,650,000 cash sheet business account and CR £1,650,000 client ledger business account.

D. CR £1,650,000 cash sheet client account and DR £1,650,000 client ledger business account.

E. CR £1,650,000 cash sheet client account and DR £1,650,000 client ledger client account.

QUESTION 4

A solicitor acts for the personal representatives in the administration of an estate. At the end of the period of administration, the residuary beneficiary (who is also one of the personal representatives) asks the solicitor to retain the £350,000 residue for six months as she is planning to emigrate to a different country next year. In the meantime, the residuary beneficiary asks the solicitor to use some of the money to pay her monthly credit card bill.

What action should the solicitor take with respect to the £350,000?

A. The solicitor should transfer the £350,000 into a separate designated deposit client account in the name of the residuary beneficiary and make the credit card payments as requested.

B. The solicitor should retain the £350,000 in the general client account and make the credit card payments as requested.

C. The solicitor should pay a large lump sum to the residuary beneficiary but retain sufficient funds in the general client account to make the monthly credit card payments until the residuary beneficiary emigrates.

D. The solicitor should transfer the £350,000 to a separate designated deposit client account in the name of the residuary beneficiary so that it is available to finance her emigration in due course. However, in the meantime, the solicitor should advise the residuary beneficiary to pay her own monthly credit card bills.

E. The solicitor should pay the residuary beneficiary the entire sum of £350,000 so that she can make the monthly credit card payments herself.

QUESTION 5

A solicitor is acting in a probate matter and needs to pay several legacies to beneficiaries in accordance with the terms of the will.

How should the solicitor pay these legacies?

A. The solicitor should pay these legacies from the business account, making accounting entries in the petty cash sheet and client ledger.

B. The solicitor should pay these legacies from the business account, making accounting entries in the cash sheet and client ledger.

C. The solicitor cannot pay these legacies until the estate accounts are approved and the distribution of assets is complete.

D. The solicitor should pay these legacies from the client account, providing there is sufficient credit balance to do so, making accounting entries in the cash sheet and client ledger.

E. The solicitor should pay these legacies from the client account, unless there is an insufficient credit balance to do so, in which case any shortfall can be paid from the business account.

■ ANSWERS TO QUESTIONS

Answers to 'What do you know already?' questions at the start of the chapter

1) False. Although the general principle in Rule 2.4 is that client money must be available on demand (ie held in an instant access account so that it can be returned to a client or third party as requested), Rule 2.4 also provides an exception so that the client and firm can have a written agreement to do something different. For example, an agreement could provide that a client's money is held on deposit instead.

2) Rule 2.5 provides that client money must be returned promptly to the client or third party when there is no longer any proper reason for holding it (eg at the end of a legal matter).

3) Rule 3.3 prohibits law firms from using their client accounts to provide banking facilities to clients or third parties. This is because client accounts must only be used to facilitate the provision of legal services, as authorised by the Solicitors Regulation Authority.

4) False. Money sent by a client to cover a disbursement that has already been paid by the firm is not client money as it does not fall within the categories of money defined as client money in Rule 2.1. It is therefore business money and should be paid into the firm's business account. If it is paid into the client account, the firm will be in breach of the Rule 4.1 requirement to keep client money separate from business money.

5) The double entry for a withdrawal from client account is:
    - DR (debit) client ledger client account; and
    - CR (credit) cash sheet client account.

Answers to end-of-chapter SQE1-style questions

Question 1:
    The correct answer was C. The cheque is *business money* because it is to *reimburse a disbursement that has already been paid from*

the business account. This is the case even before a bill is delivered (the Rules provide that money held on account of costs and *unpaid* disbursements prior to delivery of a bill is client money – this does not cover disbursements that have already been paid). Options A and B are incorrect because there is no need for the solicitor to deliver a bill before the cheque is paid into the business account. Option B also illustrates poor practice as cheques should be paid in at the bank promptly (required under the Rules for client money but also advisable for business money). Options D and E are both incorrect because the cheque is *not client money* (and for option D, the money should not be paid into the client account). Watch out for options that suggest client money should be paid into the business account (option E), or vice versa, as these are likely to be incorrect.

Question 2:

The correct answer was A. This is because if the solicitor completes the purchase before the sale proceeds are received on the sale, the purchase matter client ledger will show a debit balance on the client account. This is a breach of the Rules because other clients' funds in the general client account have been used to fund this client's purchase. To remedy the breach, the solicitor should transfer sufficient business money to clear the debit balance. Once the proceeds from the sale are received, this money can be returned to the business account. Option B is incorrect because the client ledger will have a debit rather than a credit balance and therefore the solicitor must take action to remedy the breach of the Rules. Option C is incorrect because the client and business accounts are mixed up. Option D is incorrect because the client ledger will not show a zero balance on the client account. Option E is incorrect because if the solicitor were to transfer client money from the sale ledger to the purchase ledger, there would then be a debit balance on the sale ledger, which would be just as serious a breach of the Rules. Watch out for questions where too much client money is withdrawn when there are insufficient funds in the client ledger client account. This will always be a breach of the Rules because other clients' money will have been used wrongly.

Question 3:

The correct answer was E. This is because a withdrawal of client money from the client account requires a credit (CR) entry in the cash sheet and a debit (DR) entry in the client ledger. As the transaction involves client money, the entries must be in the client account columns of both ledgers. Option A is incorrect because the profit costs ledger is not relevant to this type of transaction. Option B is incorrect because it shows the accounting entries for a receipt of money into the client account rather than a payment of money out of the client account (ie the debit and credit are the wrong way around). Option C is incorrect for the same reason as option B, but it is also incorrect because it refers to the business account rather than the client account (the net proceeds of sale are client money so the entries must be in the client account columns). Option D is incorrect because although the cash sheet entry is correct, the client ledger entry refers to the business account rather than the client account. Watch out for options that show one entry in the client account columns and one in the business account columns as they will always be incorrect, and you can discount them.

Question 4:

The correct answer was E. The residue of the estate is client money. There is no longer any proper reason (ie a reason associated with the provision of legal services) to retain the £350,000, so it must be returned to the client promptly in accordance with the Rules. All the other options are incorrect as they involve a retention of some (option C) or all of the money (options A, B and D) where there is no longer any proper reason associated with the provision of legal services to hold it. If the firm pays the monthly credit card bills (options A, B and C), this would also be a breach of the prohibition in the Rules on providing banking facilities.

Question 5:

The correct answer was D. The payment of legacies are payments of client money and there should be accounting entries in the client ledger and cash sheet (client columns in both ledgers) accordingly to record this. The legacies should not be paid unless there is a sufficient credit balance in the client account to do so, and this is the purpose for which the money is held. Therefore, option E is incorrect as there is insufficient credit balance in the client account for the probate matter. Options A and B are both incorrect because they suggest that the legacies should be paid using business money from the business account. Option C is incorrect as legacies can be paid to beneficiaries prior to the final distribution of the estate, providing there are sufficient client assets to do so without jeopardising payment of any liabilities or expenses of the estate.

■ KEY RULES

The SRA Accounts Rules 2019 can be found on the SRA website.

The SQE1 Assessment Specification for Solicitors' Accounts does not require you to know individual Rule numbers, just the principles underpinning the Rules. However, you should familiarise yourself with the operation of:
- Rule 2.4
- Rule 2.5
- Rule 3.3
- Rule 4.1
- Rule 5.1
- Rule 5.2
- Rule 5.3

Interest

■ MAKE SURE YOU KNOW

This chapter is structured around elements of the SQE1 Assessment Specification relating to the requirement to pay interest on client money and the accounting entries required. It includes the following topics:

> Requirement to pay interest on client money
>
> • Methods for dealing with interest

> Money held in the general client account
>
> • Accounting entries required

> Money held in a separate designated deposit client account
>
> • Accounting entries required

■ SQE ASSESSMENT ADVICE

As you work through this chapter, remember to pay particular attention in your revision to:
- the general principle requiring firms to account to clients or third parties for a *fair sum of interest* on any *client money* held on their behalf (Rule 7.1)
- the exception to this general principle (Rule 7.2)
- the two common situations in which a requirement to pay interest to a client may arise:
  - money held for a client in the general client bank account;
  - money held for a client in a separate designated deposit client account
- accounting entries for interest arising from *client money* held in the *general client bank account*
- accounting entries for interest arising from *client money* held in a *separate designated deposit client account* for a specific client.

■ WHAT DO YOU KNOW ALREADY?

Have a go at these questions before reading this chapter. If you find some difficult or cannot remember the answers, make a note to look more closely at that during your revision.

1) True or false? A firm must always pay interest to a client when it holds money on their behalf.

   [Requirement to pay interest on client money, page 54]

2) True or false? The payment of sums in lieu of interest to clients for monies held on their behalf in the general client account is treated as an expense of the firm.

   [Money held in the general client account, page 59]

3) What accounting entries are required when a firm pays a sum in lieu of interest to a client for monies held for that client in the general client account?

   [Accounting entries – money held in the general client account, page 59]

4) Where a firm operates a separate designated deposit client account to hold money on behalf of a specific client, how much of the interest arising from this account should be paid to the client?

   [Money held in a separate designated deposit client account, page 63]

5) What accounting entries are required to record a transfer of monies, including interest, from a separate designated deposit client account to the general client account?

   [Accounting entries for money held in an SDDCA, page 64]

REQUIREMENT TO PAY INTEREST ON CLIENT MONEY

Firms often hold *client money* on behalf of clients or others while providing legal services. Throughout this chapter, the word 'client' will be used to encompass third parties as well.

Firms may earn interest on money held in the firm's bank accounts, both on *business money* held in *business bank accounts* and *client money* held in *client bank accounts*. Although it is fair for firms to keep the interest earned on business money (their own money), it is not fair for them to keep all the interest earned on client money. Therefore, the SRA Accounts Rules ('the Rules' – see **Chapter 1**) require firms to account to clients for interest earned on client money in certain contexts.

Rule 7.1 provides that 'you account to clients or third parties for a *fair sum of interest* on any client money held by you on their behalf'. This means that where a firm holds a large sum of money for a client over a long period of time, it is fair to pay the client either *the actual interest earned* (for example, if the money is held in a **separate designated deposit client account (SDDCA)**) or to pay them some money *instead* of interest (paying a **sum in lieu of interest** on money held in the general client account). Where a firm holds a small sum of money for a client over a short period of time, it is considered fair not to pay the client any interest at all.

Key term: separate designated deposit client account (SDDCA)

This book uses 'separate designated deposit client account' to describe an account that a firm may open for an individual client, for example, if it is holding large sums of money for this client over a long period of time while providing them with legal services. SDDCA is used for an account that:
- is *separate* from the general client account;
- is *designated* in the name of an individual client;
- is a *deposit* account which will earn more interest on the client's money than if it was held in the general client account; and
- is labelled as a 'client' account in accordance with Rule 3.2(b) (see **Chapter 2**).

SDDCAs may also be known by other terms or labels (see **Revision tip, page 64**).

Key term: sum in lieu of interest

Sometimes a firm does not pay a client the *actual* interest earned on client money held on their behalf in the general client account. Instead, it applies its interest policy to decide what amount is *fair* and pays a *sum in lieu of interest* to the client (literally, a sum instead of interest).

Table 4.1 summarises the general principle requiring firms to pay a fair sum of interest to clients when holding client money on their behalf, and the exception criteria needed to justify not doing so.

Table 4.1: Requirement to pay interest

General principle – Rule 7.1	Requirement to pay a *fair sum of interest* when holding client money
Exception – Rule 7.2	If the firm provides sufficient information to the client(s) in advance, it can agree alternative arrangements with the client(s) with respect to interest. Such an agreement must be in writing

When applying Rule 7.1, a firm must decide whether to pay interest to a client at all, and if so, what rate of interest would be fair. There is nothing in the Rules to explain what '*fair*' means and the SRA has not issued guidance on this. However, previous versions of the Rules offer some helpful insights into how 'fair' is likely to be interpreted, for example:
1) Firms should have a written policy on how interest is calculated on client money and must inform their clients accordingly.
2) The policy should take account of both the amount of client money held for any client and the length of period for which it is held.

3) In deciding what rate of interest is fair, a firm should consider what rates of interest are being offered by banks and building societies. As client money must be available on demand (Rule 2.4), firms should consider the rates of interest payable on instant access accounts. They should adopt a rate that is 'fair' in the sense that it is neither the lowest nor the highest interest rate available but is somewhere in between.

4) Firms will usually have a **'de minimis'** provision under which they will not pay interest to a client. This used to be £20 but firms may use a higher threshold now, providing it is fair.

Key term: 'de minimis'

A de minimis provision is a minimum threshold. In the context of interest payments, a firm may choose not to make interest payments to any client if their entitlement to interest under the firm policy is below a certain minimum threshold (usually £20).

Practice example 4.1 illustrates how an SQE1 assessment question might test your understanding of a firm's obligations to pay interest to clients.

Practice example 4.1

A solicitor drafts a residential tenancy for a client. During the matter, the client pays £200 on account of costs and disbursements, which is held in the client account until it is needed.

Is the firm required to pay interest on the money held in client account for this client?

The firm is unlikely to pay interest to the client in this matter. This is because only a small amount of client money has been held and therefore any interest attributable is likely to fall below the de minimis provision contained in the firm's interest policy. This is *fair* because the logistics and administration involved in calculating and paying out very small amounts of interest to multiple clients would be disproportionate to the benefit to the clients of receiving such small sums.

Sometimes it is necessary to hold a large sum of client money on behalf of a specific client over a long period as part of the firm's delivery of legal services to that client. However, firms must be very careful to check that the reason for holding the money is justifiable. If not, they may be in danger of breaching the following Rules:

• Rule 2.5: 'You ensure that client money is returned promptly to the client ... as soon as there is no longer any proper reason to hold those funds.' A proper reason would be one that requires the use of the money in the firm's provision of legal services to the client. Firms must therefore return client money promptly at the end of a matter, or if there is a significant delay or change in plans which mean that the money is not needed in the short term to progress a legal matter. The client can then manage their own money and pay it back to the firm as and when it is required (see **Chapter 3**).

- Rule 3.3: 'You must not use a client account to provide banking facilities to clients ... Payments into, and transfers or withdrawals from a client account must be in respect of the delivery by you of regulated services.' Firms cannot hold money for clients unless it is needed for a legal matter and cannot accept instructions from clients for payments, transfers or withdrawals of client money that relate to non-legal matters (see **Chapter 3**).

Exam warning

If an SQE1 question relates to a large sum of client money held in a client account over a long period, check the purpose for which the money is held.

- If there is a justifiable purpose for holding the money that is related to the firm's provision of legal services, the correct answer is likely to relate to Rule 7.1, fair interest payments (see **Requirement to pay interest on client money, page 54**).
- If there is no good reason for holding the money, the firm may be in breach of Rule 2.5 and/or Rule 3.3. The correct answer would therefore be that the firm must remedy the breach promptly (in compliance with Rule 6.1 – see **Chapter 3**) by returning the money to the client, possibly with some interest.

Practice example 4.2 illustrates how your understanding of this topic might be tested in an SQE1 assessment question.

Practice example 4.2

A solicitor acts for the executors in a probate matter, one of whom is the sole beneficiary of the estate. The sole beneficiary/executor asks the solicitor to retain the money from the estate in the general client account for the time being, as she has not decided what she wants to do with the money. Four months later, she instructs the solicitor to transfer £4,000 to a travel agent for a global trip she has just booked.

How should the solicitor deal with the money from the estate?

The solicitor should have sent all money from the estate to the sole beneficiary promptly on completion of the probate matter. He should not pay any money to the travel agent. By keeping the money in client account when it is no longer needed in connection with a legal matter, the solicitor is in breach of Rule 2.5. The solicitor is also in danger of providing banking facilities to the client, particularly if he pays £4,000 to the travel agent (breach of Rule 3.3).

Methods for dealing with interest on client money

If a firm decides a client is eligible for interest arising from monies held on their behalf, it can either:

- *transfer* the interest into the client account to offset against the firm's bill or to use towards future disbursements – this is common when a legal matter is not yet completed; or
- *pay* the interest direct to the client, for example, after the end of a legal matter – this is usually through a direct transfer to the client (or via a cheque) from the business bank account.

A firm may have several client accounts at the bank – the *general client account* (defined in **Chapter 2**), which contains client money belonging to most of its clients; and several *SDDCAs* for individual clients (where a legal matter requires the firm to hold a large sum of money for an individual client for a long period of time). It may transfer money between the general client account and the SDDCAs as needed (see **Figure 4.1**). Interest may be earned on both the general client account (usually at a low rate) and on the SDDCAs (usually at a higher rate).

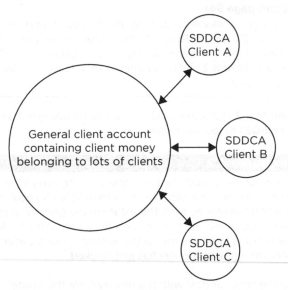

Figure 4.1: General client account and SDDCAs

The firm will deal with the interest earned on client money in two different ways, depending on where the client money is held:

1) If the money is held in the general client account, the firm will pay a *sum in lieu of interest* to the client.

2) If the money is held in an SDDCA for a specific client, the firm will usually pay the client *all interest* arising from the funds in that account.

Each of these two methods will be considered in more detail in the next sections.

MONEY HELD IN THE GENERAL CLIENT ACCOUNT

A firm will have several bank accounts, including at least one general client account, so that it can keep *client money* belonging to clients separate from *business money* belonging to the firm (Rule 4.1 – see **Chapter 2**). The general client account (often just called '*the* client account' or simply 'client account') contains money held on behalf of all, or at least most, of the firm's clients. The balance on the client account is normally high, especially for big commercial firms. A firm can earn interest on the client account, particularly as it can place a proportion of the money on deposit to earn higher rates of interest (being mindful that client money must be available on demand under Rule 2.4). This interest belongs to the firm and may be at more attractive interest rates due to the high balances involved. This interest is a source of *income* for the firm and is paid into the business bank account.

However, the firm must then pay *sums in lieu of interest* (sums instead of interest) to certain clients to comply with Rule 7.1, that is, where the firm policy determines that it is fair to do so. Such payments of sums in lieu of interest are treated as an *expense* of the firm and are recorded in an **interest payable** ledger.

Key term: interest payable
Interest payable is an expense of the firm. Each time a firm pays a sum in lieu of interest to a client, the payment is recorded in the interest payable expense ledger.

Firms usually find that they receive more *income* in the form of interest on their general client accounts than they pay out as interest payable *expenses* when paying sums in lieu of interest to clients. In this way, firms often make an *income profit* from interest earned on the general client account.

The following sections use examples to illustrate how Rule 7.1 may be applied in principle. However, please note that the interest figures may not be realistic, as interest rates are very low at the time of writing.

Accounting entries – money held in the general client account

There are two steps involved in paying the client a sum in lieu of interest arising from client money held in the general client account:

1) recording interest payable as business money; and

2) transferring a sum in lieu of interest from the business account to the client account.

Step one – recording interest payable as business money

The firm will use its interest policy to determine what sum should be paid to a client in lieu of interest. The double entry for the interest payable is then recorded in the ledgers:
- Credit (CR) client ledger business account.
- Debit (DR) interest payable (expense) ledger (this ledger only has business columns).

Exam warning

If an SQE1 assessment question asks about the accounting entries required to record interest payable as an expense, avoid options that refer to the cash sheet. Remember that there are *no* accounting entries in the *cash sheet* at step one.

Recording interest payable as an expense is illustrated in **Practice example 4.3**, showing how this topic might be assessed in the SQE1 assessment.

Practice example 4.3

A solicitor acts for a client in a commercial property transaction. As a result of the amount of money held on behalf of this client in the general client account over the course of the matter, the firm applies its interest policy and calculates that a sum in lieu of interest of £80 should be paid to the client.

What ledger entries are required to record this £80 interest payable expense?

Credit (CR) £80 client ledger business account and Debit (DR) £80 interest payable ledger. The sum in lieu of interest is an expense of the business and must be recorded in the interest payable expense ledger as a debit. The corresponding credit entry will appear in the business account columns of the client ledger.

The following case study shows how an interest payable expense is recorded in the firm's ledgers.

Example ledger entries for recording interest payable as business money

Your firm is instructed by Okoro Properties Ltd in a high value commercial property transaction. At the end of the matter, you assess that the client is entitled to a sum of £500 in lieu of interest due to the high level of monies held in general client account, and the period for which they were held. The double entry to record the interest payable expense is highlighted in italics in the two ledgers shown in **Figure 4.2**.

Client ledger: Okoro Properties Ltd (extract) Matter: Purchase of Grange Wharf Plots 1–10							
		Business account			Client account		
Date	Details	DR	CR	Bal	DR	CR	Bal
	Existing balances			XX			XX
	Interest payable		*500*	XX			XX

Interest payable ledger (extract)				
Date	Details	DR	CR	Bal
	Existing balances			XX
	Okoro Properties Ltd: Purchase of Grange Wharf Plots 1–10	*500*		XX

Figure 4.2: Ledger entries for recording interest payable as business money

Step two – transferring a sum in lieu of interest from the business account to the client account

As the interest payable is an expense of the business (recorded in the business account columns), the sum in lieu of interest for a client must be transferred from the business bank account to the client bank account (business to client cash transfer – see **Chapter 6, Cash transfers, page 111**, for more details). This involves two related pairs of double entries as follows:

1) Transfer the sum in lieu of interest *out of the business account*:
   - DR client ledger business account.
   - CR cash sheet business account.
2) Transfer the sum in lieu of interest *into the client account*:
   - CR client ledger client account.
   - DR cash sheet client account.

Usually, both pairs of entries are recorded on the same lines of the respective ledgers (transfer out of business account; and transfer into client account). However, some firms may record the double entries over two separate lines. *No entries are made in the interest payable ledger at step two.*

Example ledger entries for transferring a sum in lieu of interest from the business to the client account

This example continues the Okoro Properties Ltd case study introduced previously. Once the interest payable entries have been recorded, the sum in lieu of interest must be transferred from the business to the client account. The double entries for the business to client transfer are shown in italics in the ledgers in **Figure 4.3**.

Client ledger: Okoro Properties Ltd (extract) Matter: Purchase of Grange Wharf Plots 1–10							
		Business account			Client account		
Date	Details	DR	CR	Bal	DR	CR	Bal
	Existing balances			XX			XX
	Interest payable		500	XX			XX
	Cash – transfer of sum in lieu of interest from business to client account	*500*		XX		*500*	XX

Cash sheet (extract)							
		Business account			Client account		
Date	Details	DR	CR	Bal	DR	CR	Bal
	Existing balances			XX			XX
	Okoro Properties Ltd: Purchase of Grange Wharf Plots 1–10 – transfer of sum in lieu of interest from business to client account		*500*	XX	*500*		XX

Figure 4.3: Ledger entries to transfer a sum in lieu of interest from the business to the client account

Interest payable ledger (extract)				
Date	Details	DR	CR	Bal
	Existing balance			XX
	Okoro Properties Ltd: Purchase of Grange Wharf Plots 1–10	500		XX

Figure 4.3: (continued)

Practice example 4.4 illustrates how the SQE1 assessment might test your understanding of how a firm accounts to a client for a sum in lieu of interest. This example incorporates both steps involved, although other questions might focus on one step only.

Practice example 4.4

A solicitor has just completed the administration of a high value estate. During the administration period, the firm has held significant sums of client money in the general client account in this matter. Therefore, using the firm's interest policy, the solicitor assesses that the client is entitled to a sum in lieu of interest of £250.

How will the firm record the payment of this sum in lieu of interest in the client ledger?

The client ledger will show a credit receipt of £250 in the business account, followed by a transfer of this sum from business account to client account (DR client ledger business account and CR client ledger client account).

MONEY HELD IN A SEPARATE DESIGNATED DEPOSIT CLIENT ACCOUNT

If a firm holds large sums of money for a specific client over a long period of time, it may be in the best interests of the client for the money to be transferred out of the general client account and into an SDDCA where it can earn higher rates of interest on deposit (however, remember that an SDDCA should not be used to provide banking facilities to clients as this would be a breach of Rule 3.3).

The SDDCA should be an instant access deposit account to comply with the requirement that client money is available on demand (Rule 2.4) unless the firm has agreed an alternative arrangement in writing with a client. For example, a firm may agree with a client to hold their money in a deposit account with a notice period for withdrawals as this may offer higher interest rates. This is permitted by Rule 2.4.

Revision tip

The SQE1 assessment may use different terminology for an SDDCA so you should be aware of alternative wording such as:
- Separate designated client accounts.
- Separate designated deposit bank accounts.
- Designated deposit accounts.

When client money is held in an SDDCA, *all the interest arising from the account should be paid to the client.*

Most SDDCAs do not allow direct payments to be made out of the account. Therefore, when the money in an SDDCA is needed, it is usual for the sums held, plus any interest arising, to be transferred into the general client account. This money can then be paid out from the general client account, whenever it is needed, to progress the legal matter for which it was being held.

There are three stages involved in this process:
1) The client money is transferred from the general client account into an SDDCA where it can be held on deposit for a specific client.
2) The bank pays interest on the client money held on deposit in the SDDCA.
3) The client money, including interest accrued, is transferred back into the general client account from the SDDCA.

Accounting entries for money held in an SDDCA

There are two methods of recording ledger entries when accounting to clients for interest on money held on their behalf in an SDDCA:
1) extra columns on existing ledgers for money on deposit; or
2) separate ledgers for money on deposit.

There is no difference in what happens at the bank, that is, the client's money is still held separately from the general client account in an SDDCA, it is just the method of recording this in the firm's ledgers that is different. Each method will be considered in more detail below.

Extra columns for money on deposit

If this method is used, the existing client ledger and cash sheet will have three extra columns on the right-hand side as illustrated in italics on the ledgers in **Figure 4.4**.

Client ledger: Matter:									
		Business account			Client account			*Client deposit*		
Date	Details	DR	CR	Bal	DR	CR	Bal	*DR*	*CR*	*Bal*

Cash sheet									
		Business account			Client account			*Client deposit*		
Date	Details	DR	CR	Bal	DR	CR	Bal	*DR*	*CR*	*Bal*

Figure 4.4: Example client ledger and cash sheet showing the three extra columns for client money held on deposit

The journal entries for using the extra column method to record interest earned on client money in an SDDCA would usually involve three stages requiring double entries as shown in **Figure 4.5**.

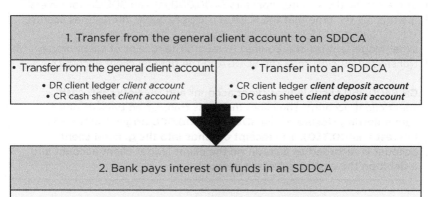

Figure 4.5: Journal entries using the extra columns method

This may be easier to understand when you see the entries on the ledgers themselves as shown in the following case study.

Example ledger entries using the extra columns method

You act for the executors of Baleen Singh, who was extremely wealthy. During the probate period there are justifiable reasons for holding £500,000 in an SDDCA for several months without breaching any of the Rules. The money earns £850 interest while in the SDDCA. When the SDDCA is closed, £500,850 (original sum + interest) is transferred back into the general client account so that it can be distributed to the beneficiaries.

The ledgers in **Figure 4.6** show the double entries for each of the three stages.

In the SQE1 assessment, you may have a question which asks you about just one of these stages rather than all of them, as illustrated in **Practice example 4.5**.

Practice example 4.5

A solicitor acts for a client in a probate matter. During the administration of the estate, the solicitor transfers £400,000 into an SDDCA for several months. By the time that the SDDCA is closed, £350 interest has accrued.

What ledger entries are required to record the receipt of client money transferred on closure of the SDDCA to the general client account?

CR £400,350 client ledger client account and DR £400,350 cash sheet client account. The client money is transferred back as one sum following closure of the SDDCA (£400,000 original sum + £350 interest = £400,350). The receipt of funds into the general client account is recorded as a credit on the client ledger client account and a debit on the cash sheet client account.

Separate ledgers for money on deposit

If this method is used, there will be four different ledgers involved in recording the transfer of client money to and from an SDDCA, including interest earned on client money while held in the SDDCA:

• Two client ledgers for the client:
  - Client ledger (as normal).
  - Deposit client ledger.
• Two cash sheets:
  - Cash sheet (as normal).
  - Deposit cash sheet.

The journal entries for using the separate ledger method to record interest earned on client money in an SDDCA would usually involve three stages

1 Jan	Firm transfers £500,000 from general client account to an SDDCA
2 April	Bank pays interest of £850 arising on monies in an SDDCA
2 April	Firm transfers £500,850 (original money + interest) back from an SDDCA to the general client account

Client ledger: Executors of Baleen Singh deceased (extract)
Matter: Probate

Date	Details	Business account			Client account			Client deposit		
		DR	CR	Bal	DR	CR	Bal	DR	CR	Bal
	Existing balances			XX			XX			
1/1	Cash – transfer from client to client deposit			XX	500,000		XX		500,000	500,000 CR
2/4	Deposit cash – interest			XX			XX		850	500,850 CR
2/4	Cash – transfer from client deposit to client			XX		500,850	XX	500,850		–

Figure 4.6: Ledger entries to record interest earned on an SDDCA, using the extra columns method

Cash sheet (extract)

Date	Details	Business account			Client account			Client deposit		
		DR	CR	Bal	DR	CR	Bal	DR	CR	Bal
	Existing balances			XX			XX			XX
1/1	Baleen Singh probate – transfer from client to client deposit			XX		500,000	XX	500,000		XX
2/4	Baleen Singh probate deposit – interest			XX			XX	850		XX
2/4	Baleen Singh probate – transfer from client deposit to client			XX	500,850		XX		500,850	XX

Figure 4.6: (continued)

requiring double entries, as shown in **Figure 4.7**. You will note that the journal entries are similar to those shown in **Figure 4.5**. However, in **Figure 4.5** there are no references to separate ledgers (*deposit client ledger and deposit cash sheet*).

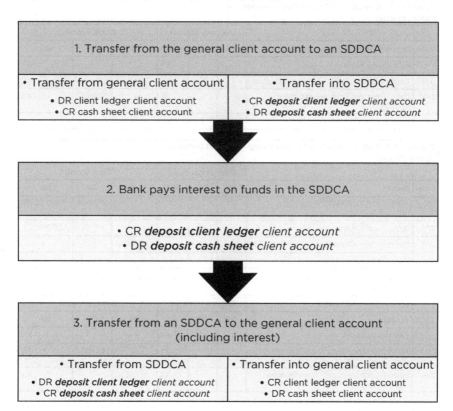

Figure 4.7: Journal entries using the separate ledger method

This may be easier to understand when you see the entries on the ledgers themselves. The example shown in **Figure 4.8** uses the same case study relating to the probate of Baleen Singh deceased, but shows the ledger entries using the *separate ledger method*.

The ledgers in **Figure 4.8** show the double entries for each of the three stages.

Practice example 4.6 illustrates how your understanding of this topic might be assessed in the SQE1 assessment.

1 Jan	Firm transfers £500,000 from the general client account to an SDDCA
2 April	Bank pays interest of £850 arising on monies in the SDDCA
2 April	Firm transfers £500,850 (original money + interest) back from the SDDCA to the general client account

Client ledger: Executors of Baleen Singh deceased (extract)
Matter: Probate

		Business account			Client account		
Date	Details	DR	CR	Bal	DR	CR	Bal
	Existing balances			XX			XX
1/1	Cash – transfer to deposit client account			XX	500,000		XX
2/4	Cash – transfer from deposit client account			XX		500,850	XX

Deposit client ledger: Executors of Baleen Singh deceased (extract)
Matter: Probate

		Business account			Client account		
Date	Details	DR	CR	Bal	DR	CR	Bal
1/1	Deposit cash – transfer from client account					500,000	500,000 CR
2/4	Deposit cash – interest					850	500,850 CR
2/4	Deposit cash – transfer to client account				500,850		–

Cash sheet (extract)

		Business account			Client account		
Date	Details	DR	CR	Bal	DR	CR	Bal
	Existing balances			XX			XX
1/1	Baleen Singh probate – transfer to deposit account			XX		500,000	XX
2/4	Baleen Singh probate – transfer from deposit account			XX	500,850		XX

Deposit cash sheet (extract)

		Business account			Client account		
Date	Details	DR	CR	Bal	DR	CR	Bal
	Existing balances			XX			XX
1/1	Baleen Singh probate deposit – transfer from client account			XX	500,000		XX
2/4	Baleen Singh probate deposit – interest			XX	850		XX
2/4	Baleen Singh probate deposit – transfer to client account			XX		500,850	XX

Figure 4.8: Ledger entries to record interest earned on SDDCA, using the separate ledger method

Practice example 4.6

A solicitor acts for a client in a commercial property transaction. During the transaction, she transfers £250,000 of the client's money into an SDDCA for several months until it is required to complete the property purchase, at which point she transfers the funds back into the general client account. Interest of £500 is accrued on the SDDCA during this period.

What ledger entries are required to record the accrual of interest on the SDDCA?

This question addresses stage 2 of the full interest transaction, that is, the journal entries for adding the interest to the SDDCA.

The SQE1 assessment might present the correct answer using the separate ledger method – CR £500 *deposit client ledger* client account and DR £500 *deposit cash sheet* client account.

Alternatively, the SQE1 assessment might present the correct answer using the extra columns method – CR £500 client ledger *client deposit account* and DR £500 cash sheet *client deposit account*.

Revision tip

The series of entries required for a full transaction involving money held in an SDDCA, and the interest arising from it, are probably too complex to be assessed on the SQE1 assessment in a single question. However, you may need to identify the correct explanation for how firms account to clients for interest in a particular context, or to identify the correct ledger entries for one part of an interest transaction.

■ KEY POINT CHECKLIST

This chapter has covered the following key knowledge points. You can structure your revision around these, making sure you recall the key details for each point, as covered in this chapter.

- The requirement for firms to pay clients a *fair sum of interest* on *client money* held on their behalf.
- The exception that allows firms to agree, in writing, different interest arrangements with clients, after provision of sufficient information.
- Firms must not hold money for clients unless it is necessary for the provision of legal services, or they may be in breach of the *duty to return client money promptly* when it is no longer needed or the important *prohibition on providing banking facilities* to clients.

- Interest arising from the *general client account* belongs to the firm and is therefore *business money*. However, a firm should pay a *fair sum in lieu of interest* to a client where it is fair to do so.
- *Interest payable* (for sums in lieu of interest for client money held in the general client account) is treated as an *expense* of the firm.
- There are two stages for accounting to clients for sums in lieu of interest on client money held in the general client account:
    1) Recording interest payable as business money (DR interest payable ledger and CR client ledger business account).
    2) Transferring a sum in lieu of interest from the business account to the client account:
        a) transfer from business account (DR client ledger business account and CR cash sheet business account); and
        b) transfer to client account (CR client ledger client account and DR cash sheet client account).
- If client money is transferred to an SDDCA, the firm should pay the client *all interest* arising on that account.
- There are three stages in accounting to clients for interest arising from client money held in an SDDCA:
    1) Transfer from general client account to an SDDCA.
    2) Receipt of interest on an SDDCA.
    3) Transfer from an SDDCA to the general client account (including interest).
- There are two methods for recording the ledger entries to account for interest arising from client money held in an SDDCA:
    1) Extra columns method (see **Figure 4.5**).
    2) Separate ledgers method (see **Figure 4.7**).

■ KEY TERMS AND CONCEPTS

- separate designated deposit client account (SDDCA) (**page 55**)
- sum in lieu of interest (**page 55**)
- de minimis (**page 56**)
- interest payable (**page 59**)

■ SQE1-STYLE QUESTIONS

QUESTION 1

A client instructs a law firm in the sale of her home. The net proceeds of sale are currently in the firm's general client account. The client intends to use these monies to buy a new home at some point in the future, but in the meantime she is living in an apartment in Paris. She instructs the firm to retain the net proceeds of sale in order to pay the rent on the apartment on her behalf until further notice.

Which of the following best describes what the firm should do?

A. The firm should retain the net proceeds of sale in the general client account and pay the apartment rent as requested. When the client requests the return of any remaining proceeds of sale, the firm should also account to the client for a sum in lieu of interest if appropriate under the firm's interest policy.

B. The firm should transfer the net proceeds of sale to a separate designated deposit client account (SDDCA) but transfer regular amounts back to the general client account in order to cover the rental payments. The firm should also account to the client for any interest earned on the SDDCA.

C. The firm should transfer the net proceeds of sale to an SDDCA until the client requests its use towards the purchase of a new home. The firm should pay the client any interest arising from the sums held in the SDDCA.

D. The firm should pay the net proceeds of sale to the client as soon as possible so that she can pay the rent on her apartment herself.

E. The firm should retain the net proceeds of sale in the general client account until the client instructs the firm in the purchase of a new home. The firm should account to the client for a sum in lieu of interest if appropriate under the firm's interest policy. The firm should also advise the client to pay the rent on her apartment direct from her income.

QUESTION 2

A firm holds money for its clients in its general client bank account, on which it earns interest.

Which of the following best describes how the firm should deal with this interest?

A. The firm should pay its clients the exact amount of interest attributable to monies held on their behalf in the general client account.

B. The firm can retain any interest earned on the general client account and should only account to clients for interest earned on monies held in a separate designated deposit client account.

C. The firm should pay its clients the exact amount of interest attributable to monies held on their behalf in the general client account, subject to a de minimis provision.

D. The firm must pay its clients a fair sum in lieu of interest unless it has informed its clients that interest will be paid under different arrangements.

E. The firm should pay its clients a fair sum in lieu of interest, subject to any de minimis provision or alternative arrangements agreed in writing with any client(s).

QUESTION 3

A firm holds money for a client in the general client account while acting for him in a commercial property transaction. On completion of the matter, the firm applies its interest policy and calculates that it owes him a sum of £52 in lieu of interest. This sum will be offset against the firm's profit costs once a bill is delivered at the end of the matter.

Which of the following best describes how the firm should account to the client for this sum in lieu of interest?

A. The sum in lieu of interest belongs to the client so the firm should pay it directly into the client bank account, with ledger entries recorded on both the client and interest payable ledgers.

B. As interest payable is a business expense, the firm should record £52 in the client account columns of both the interest payable and client ledgers before transferring the sum from the client bank account to the business bank account.

C. As interest payable is a business expense, the firm should record £52 in both the interest payable ledger and in the business account columns of the client ledger before transferring the sum from the business bank account to the client bank account.

D. The sum of £52 will automatically be credited to the client under the firm's interest policy and there is no need to make any entries in the ledgers to record this.

E. The firm will pay the client £52 by a cheque drawn on the general client bank account.

QUESTION 4

A firm holds £100,000 for a commercial property client in a separate designated deposit client account (SDDCA), on which £200 interest has accrued. The client instructs the firm to close the SDDCA and transfer the funds back into the general client account so that it can be used towards the deposit for a new office block.

What ledger entries are required to record the receipt of funds into the general client account, following closure of the SDDCA?

A. Credit (CR) £200 client ledger business account and debit (DR) £200 cash sheet business account.

B. CR £100,000 client ledger client account and DR £100,000 cash sheet client account.

C. CR £100,000 client ledger client account and CR £200 client ledger business account.

D. CR £100,200 client ledger client account and DR £100,200 cash sheet client account.

E. CR £100,000 cash sheet client account and DR £100,000 client ledger client account.

QUESTION 5

A firm holds money for the executors of an estate in the general client account while acting for them in a probate matter. On completion of the matter, the firm applies its interest policy and calculates that it owes the estate a sum of £105 in lieu of interest. This sum must be added to the estate prior to distribution to the beneficiaries. The firm has already made the required double entry to record the interest payable as an expense of the firm.

What ledger entry(ies) should appear on the *client ledger* to complete the payment of the sum in lieu of interest to the estate?

A. Debit (DR) £105 client ledger business account and credit (CR) £105 client ledger client account.

B. DR £105 client ledger client account and CR £105 client ledger business account.

C. CR £105 client ledger client account.

D. DR £105 client ledger client account.

E. CR £105 client ledger business account.

■ ANSWERS TO QUESTIONS

Answers to 'What do you know already?' questions at the start of the chapter

1) False. Rule 7.2 provides an exception to the Rule 7.1 requirement to pay a fair sum of interest on client money. To rely on this exception, a firm must:
   - provide sufficient information to the client or third party for an informed decision; and
   - record the different arrangement for interest in a written agreement.

2) True. Sums paid to clients in lieu of interest are treated as an expense of the firm.

3) Accounting entries (journal entries) to record the payment of a sum in lieu of interest to a client for monies held on their behalf in the general client account:
   - CR client ledger business account;
   - DR interest payable ledger (remember that the interest payable ledger is an expense account of the firm and so the ledger will only have business account columns).

4) The firm should pay *all* the interest arising from monies held in a separate designated deposit client account to the client.

5) Accounting entries (journal entries) for transferring client money (including interest) from a separate designated deposit client account (SDDCA) to the general client account:
   - DR deposit client ledger client account and CR deposit cash sheet client account to transfer the money *out of* the SDDCA;
   - CR client ledger client account and DR cash sheet client account to transfer the money *into* the general client account.

Answers to end-of-chapter SQE1-style questions

Question 1:

The correct answer was D. The Rules require the firm to return client money promptly when there is no longer any proper reason for holding it. Although it may be appropriate for a firm to retain the net proceeds of sale for a short time where there is a related purchase due to complete imminently, this is not the case here. Therefore, the net proceeds of sale should be sent to the client promptly. Options C and E are therefore incorrect. Also, the Rules prohibit the firm from offering banking facilities to the client. Therefore, the firm cannot withdraw money from client account to make the rental payments on the apartment in Paris. Any such withdrawal would be unconnected to any legal services provided by the firm. Options A and B are therefore incorrect. The client must make the rental payments herself. See **Chapter 3** for more details on returning money promptly to clients and the prohibition on providing banking facilities.

Question 2:

The correct answer was E. This is because the Rules require the firm to account to clients for a fair sum of interest for money held on their behalf. It is good practice for firms to have a written policy explaining how they will calculate a fair sum in lieu of interest for monies held in the general client account (this policy will usually contain a de minimis provision). However, firms can agree an alternative arrangement in writing with their client(s), providing they have provided sufficient information to the client in advance for them to make an informed choice. Option B is wrong as although interest earned on the general client account belongs to the firm, the Rules require the firm to pay a fair sum of interest on client money whether it is held in an SDDCA or the general client account. Options A and C are not correct because many firms earn a higher rate of interest on their general client accounts than that which would be deemed fair to pay to clients. It would also be too complex and costly to account to *every* client for interest attributable to monies held on their behalf in the general client account. For many clients, the interest sums would be tiny, which is why most firms have a de minimis provision under which they do not consider it fair to pay any interest. Option D is wrong as although the Rules allow firms to reach different arrangements with clients with respect to paying interest, a firm must agree to this in writing with clients having previously given them sufficient information to make an informed choice. It is not enough to simply *inform* the clients that the firm is opting out of the obligation to pay a fair sum of interest.

Question 3:

The correct answer was C. This is because it correctly states that interest payable is a business expense and then describes the two steps involved. Step one is to record interest payable as *business* money before step two when the sum in lieu of interest is transferred from the *business* bank account to the *client* account bank account. Option B is wrong because the client and business columns are the wrong way around. Option A is wrong because it does not recognise that interest payable is *business* money and therefore cannot be paid straight into *client* account. Option D is wrong because the sum in lieu of interest will *not* be automatically credited to the *client* account. Also, there must *always* be ledger entries to record payment of a sum in lieu of interest. Option E is wrong because the question indicates that the sum in lieu of interest will be offset against the profit costs owed to the firm. A firm might decide to pay a sum in lieu of interest to a client after the completion of a matter, but, if so, it would probably use a cheque drawn on the *business* bank account or do a bank transfer direct from the *business* bank account.

Question 4:

The correct answer was D. This is because when the SDDCA was closed, the *whole sum* of £100,200 (original sum £100,000 + interest £200) should have been transferred as one payment. It must go into the client account columns as it is client money. As a *payment into* the client account, the credit entry will be on the client ledger and the debit entry will be on the cash sheet. Option A is incorrect because the amount was wrong and because it refers to the business account rather than the client account. Option B is incorrect because the amount is wrong. Option C is incorrect because the amounts do not match and are both wrong. There is also an error in the double entries because they are both credits (there should be one credit and one debit). Option E is incorrect because the amount is wrong, and the debit and credit are the wrong way around.

Question 5:

The correct answer was A. This is because the question indicates that the interest payable has already been recorded in the client ledger business account (step one). Step two requires the sum in lieu of interest to be transferred from the business account to the client account (business to client cash transfer). As the question only asks for information about the entries on the client ledger (rather than on the cash sheet as well), the client ledger will show a debit entry in the business account columns (transfer out of business account) and a credit entry in the client account columns (transfer into client account). Option B is incorrect because it shows a client to business transfer rather than a business to client transfer. Options C, D and E are all incorrect because a business to client cash transfer requires two ledger entries on the client ledger rather than just one. Option C shows only the transfer into client account correctly, whereas options D and E are completely incorrect. See **Chapter 6** for more details on cash transfers.

■ KEY RULES

The SRA Accounts Rules 2019 can be found on the SRA website.

The SQE1 Assessment Specification for Solicitors' Accounts does not require you to know individual Rule numbers, just the principles underpinning the Rules. However, you should familiarise yourself with the operation of:
• Rule 2.4
• Rule 2.5
• Rule 3.2(b)
• Rule 3.3
• Rule 7.1
• Rule 7.2

Bills

■ MAKE SURE YOU KNOW

This chapter is structured around elements of the SQE1 Assessment Specification relating to billing clients and related accounting entries. It includes the following topics:

> **Submitting a bill**
>
> • Profit costs
> • VAT
> • Accounting entries – submitting a bill

> **Reducing a bill**
>
> • Abatements
> • Accounting entries – abatements

> **Payment of a bill**
>
> • Accounting entries – payment of a bill
> • Money received on account of costs and disbursements
> • Accounting entries – money received on account
> • Money held in client account for fees

■ SQE ASSESSMENT ADVICE

As you work through this chapter, remember to pay particular attention in your revision to:
• the definitions of *profit costs* and *VAT*
• the *accounting entries* required when *submitting a bill* to a client, including the VAT element
• the requirement to keep a readily accessible *record of all bills* submitted (Rule 8.4)
• the definition of an *abatement* (bill reduction)
• the *accounting entries* required when *reducing a client's bill*
• the *payment of bills* by different methods and the related *accounting entries* required

- the recognition that money held *on account of costs and disbursements* prior to submission of a bill is *client money* and should therefore be held in a *client account* (Rule 2.1(d))
- the criteria that must be satisfied prior to transferring money from a client account to a business account to cover payment of a bill that has been submitted (Rule 4.3).

■ WHAT DO YOU KNOW ALREADY?

Have a go at these questions before reading this chapter. If you find some difficult or cannot remember the answers, make a note to look more closely at that during your revision.

1) True or false? A firm must keep a central record of all bills that is readily accessible.

   [Profit costs, page 81]

2) What are the accounting entries required when submitting a bill?

   [Accounting entries – submitting a bill, page 82]

3) True or false? There are no accounting entries required in the cash sheet when a firm submits a bill to a client.

   [Example ledger entries – submitting a bill, page 82]

4) Which of the following accounting entries are required to record the reduction in a client's bill?

   a) CR client ledger client account and DR cash sheet client account.

   b) DR client ledger business account, CR cash sheet business account and CR profit costs ledger.

   c) CR client ledger business account, DR profit costs ledger and DR HMRC-VAT ledger.

   [Example ledger entries – reducing a bill, page 84]

5) True or false? If your client sends you money towards your professional fees in accordance with a quote that you have given over the telephone, you can pay the money into your business account as soon as you receive it.

   [Payment of a bill, page 86]

SUBMITTING A BILL – PROFIT COSTS AND VAT

Law firms send bills to their clients to charge them for the legal services that the firm has provided. This is sometimes called *submitting or delivering a bill*. Firms usually submit *final bills* at the end of a matter, when the legal work that they are doing for the client is complete. However, sometimes firms submit *interim bills* at intervals during longer or more complex legal matters.

When a firm submits a bill to a client, it must charge them for both **profit costs** and **VAT**. The bill may also include charges for *disbursements* (see **Chapter 2** for the definition of disbursements and **Chapter 6** for more details on accounting entries for disbursements).

Key term: profit costs

Profit costs are sometimes called professional fees or charges. The firm will charge the client profit costs for the legal services it has provided.

Key term: VAT

VAT is Value Added Tax. VAT is a consumer tax that individuals and businesses pay when they buy goods and services. The current rate of VAT on most services, including legal services, is 20%.

Profit costs

The profit costs ledger is a record of all bills submitted by the firm. The managers of the firm will check this ledger regularly to see how much has been billed by the fee earners (the members of staff that generate income for the firm) in any given period.

Under Rule 8.4 of the SRA Accounts Rules ('the Rules' – **see Chapter 1**), the firm must keep a record of all bills (or other written notifications of costs) and this record must be readily accessible (see **Chapter 8** for more details on record keeping).

VAT

Most law firms are registered for VAT and the examples in this book reflect this. Firms must keep accurate records for VAT so that they can account to **Her Majesty's Revenue and Customs (HMRC)** for VAT as appropriate. The ledger for HMRC-VAT is a record of all the *output VAT* that the firm has charged when providing legal services to clients. It is also a record of all the *input VAT* that the firm has paid when buying the goods and services it needs to run the business. Every three months, the firm will use the records in the HMRC-VAT ledger to complete a VAT return for submission to HMRC. If the output VAT exceeds the input VAT, then the firm will be liable to pay the difference to HMRC. If the input VAT exceeds the output VAT, then HMRC will pay the firm a VAT refund (see **Chapter 6** for more details on VAT).

> **Key term: Her Majesty's Revenue and Customs (HMRC)**
>
> HMRC is the body that collects different taxes, including VAT, on behalf of the government.

Accounting entries – submitting a bill

In the SQE1 assessment, you may be required to identify the appropriate accounting entries (journal entries) required to record the submission of a bill to a client. The correct accounting entries will consist of two pairs of double entries. One double entry relates to the *profit costs* element of the bill and the other relates to the *VAT* element of the bill. You should memorise these accounting entries accordingly:

1) DR client ledger business account and CR profit costs ledger (for the profit costs element of the bill); and

2) DR client ledger business account and CR HMRC-VAT ledger (for the VAT element of the bill).

As you can see, for one bill there will be two entries on the *client ledger* (one for profit costs and one for VAT) and one entry on each of the profit costs and HMRC-VAT ledgers respectively. Both entries on the client ledger must be in the *business account columns*.

The ledgers for profit costs and HMRC-VAT only have *business account columns* (and no client account columns). This is because they are only used for transactions involving *business matters* and *business money* (see **Chapter 1** for more details of ledgers with only business account columns).

> **Exam warning**
>
> If the SQE1 assessment includes a question on submitting a bill, remember that the correct answer will *not* include any accounting entries in the *cash sheet*. This is because the client has not yet paid the bill.

Example ledger entries – submitting a bill

When revising for the SQE1 assessment, you may find it easier to memorise the accounting entries for submitting a bill if you can visualise how they appear in the relevant ledgers.

In the following case study, a firm has drafted a power of attorney for Amina Patel in accordance with her instructions. At the end of the matter, the firm submits a bill of £400 plus VAT to Amina. The ledgers in **Figure 5.1** illustrate the accounting entries required to record the submission of this bill.

Client ledger: Amina Patel (extract) Matter: Power of Attorney							
		Business account			Client account		
Date	Details	DR	CR	Bal	DR	CR	Bal
	Profit costs	400		400 DR			
	HMRC-VAT	80		480 DR			

Profit costs ledger (extract)				
Date	Details	DR	CR	Bal
	Existing balances			XX
	A Patel power of attorney – profit costs		400	XX

HMRC-VAT ledger (extract)				
Date	Details	DR	CR	Bal
	Existing balances			XX
	A Patel power of attorney – VAT		80	80 CR

Figure 5.1: Ledger entries to record submission of bill

In the SQE1 assessment, you may be required to calculate the VAT element of a bill. Remember that VAT is charged at 20% on legal services (and on some disbursements – see **Chapter 6** for more details on disbursements and VAT).

Revision tip

There are different methods for calculating VAT but they all give the same answer.

Here are some of the different methods to calculate VAT on profit costs of £100:
- Multiply the profit costs by 0.2: £100 × 0.2 = £20.
- Calculate 20% of the profit costs: £100 × 20% = £20.
- Work out one-fifth of the profit costs by dividing by 5: £100 ÷ 5 = £20.

Pick the method that makes the most sense to you and memorise it so that you can do VAT calculations quickly and reliably in the SQE assessment. You can ignore the other methods.

REDUCING A BILL - ABATEMENTS

Sometimes a law firm needs to reduce a bill for a client. This may arise because the client is dissatisfied with the legal services provided and the firm agrees a discount, or perhaps the final bill is more than the original quotation and the client asks for it to be reduced. A bill reduction is sometimes called an **abatement**.

Key term: abatement

An abatement is an agreed reduction in a client's bill.

In the SQE1 assessment, you may be required to identify the appropriate accounting entries (journal entries) required to record the abatement of a bill. The correct accounting entries will consist of two pairs of double entries. One double entry relates to the abatement of the *profit costs* element of the bill and the other relates to the abatement of the *VAT* element of the bill. You should memorise these accounting entries accordingly:

1) CR client ledger business account and DR profit costs ledger (for the abatement of the *profit costs element* of the bill); and
2) CR client ledger business account and DR HMRC-VAT ledger (for the abatement of the *VAT element* of the bill).

As you can see, for an abatement there are two entries on the client ledger business account (one for profit costs and one for VAT) and one entry on each of the profit costs and HMRC-VAT ledgers respectively. Both entries on the client ledger must be in the business account section. You will also note that although the ledgers are the same as when submitting a bill, the *debits and credits* are the *opposite way around*.

Exam warning

When reducing a bill, the accounting entries will reflect the amount of the agreed abatement, that is, what the bill has been 'reduced by' *not* what the bill has been 'reduced to'. For example, if the original bill submitted is £400 + VAT and the firm agrees a 25% abatement with the client, the accounting entries will be for £100 + VAT (the abatement) *not* £300 + VAT (the amount that the bill has been reduced to). Ledger entries for this abatement are shown in the next section.

Example ledger entries - reducing a bill

When revising for the SQE1 assessment, you may find it easier to memorise the accounting entries for reducing a bill if you can visualise how they appear in the relevant ledgers.

To illustrate the ledger entries required to record an abatement, we will continue the case study relating to Amina Patel considered above. If Amina is dissatisfied with the length of time that it has taken to draw up the power of attorney, the firm may agree to reduce her original bill of £400 + VAT to £300 + VAT. The abatement will therefore be for £100 + VAT.

The ledgers in **Figure 5.2** include the entries for the original bill, followed by the entries for the *abatement* (highlighted in italics).

Client ledger: Amina Patel (extract)
Matter: Power of Attorney

Date	Details	Business account			Client account		
		DR	CR	Bal	DR	CR	Bal
	Profit costs	400		400 DR			
	HMRC-VAT	80		480 DR			
	Profit costs (abatement)		*100*	380 DR			
	HMRC-VAT (abatement)		*20*	360 DR*			

* Note that the business account balance after the abatement is £360 DR. This reflects the reduced charge to the client of £300 + £60 VAT = £360.

Profit costs (extract)

Date	Details	DR	CR	Bal
	Existing balances			XX
	A Patel power of attorney – profit costs		400	XX
	A Patel power of attorney – profit costs (abatement)	*100*		XX

HMRC-VAT (extract)

Date	Details	DR	CR	Bal
	Existing balances			XX
	A Patel power of attorney – VAT		80	XX
	A Patel power of attorney – VAT (abatement)	*20*		XX

Figure 5.2: Ledger entries for an abatement

> **Revision tip**
>
> When reducing a bill, remember that the debits and credits are the
> opposite way round than when submitting a bill (see **Table 5.1**).

Table 5.1: Debits and credits when submitting or reducing a bill

Ledgers	Submitting a bill	Reducing a bill
Client ledger (business account columns)	DR (both profit costs element and VAT element)	CR (both profit costs element and VAT element)
Profit costs ledger	CR	DR
HMRC-VAT ledger	CR	DR

PAYMENT OF A BILL

Once a firm has submitted a bill to a client, there are different ways in which
the bill may be paid.

If a firm is not already holding money on behalf of a client in the client
account, it will expect them to make a direct payment to cover their bill.
This may be by way of bank transfer or cheque, and the receipt will be paid
directly into the business bank account (the receipt will be *business money*
rather than *client money* as a bill has already been submitted – Rule 2.1(d)).

However, a client may have already paid the firm some **money on account
of costs and disbursements**. Rule 2.1(d) provides that money 'on account'
is *client money* and must be held in the *client account* until a bill has been
submitted. However, once the client is billed, the relevant sum can be
transferred from the client account to the business account to clear what is
owed, providing there are sufficient funds available (Rule 4.3). If there is any
shortfall, the client must pay the balance owing.

Alternatively, the firm may be holding money from other sources on behalf
of the client in the client account (for example, the net proceeds of sale from
a property transaction, a financial settlement following a litigation dispute,
or monies collected in a probate matter). Once a bill has been submitted,
the client may authorise the firm to transfer the relevant sum from the client
account to the business account. However, money held in the client account
for other purposes, for example a mortgage advance, cannot be transferred
to the business account to cover fees and disbursements.

Whichever method is used to pay the bill, the receipt of money into the
business account to clear it will require the following accounting entries
(journal entries) – *CR client ledger business account and DR cash sheet
business account*. You should memorise these accounting entries so that you
can identify the correct answer on an SQE1 assessment question on this topic.

Key term: money on account of costs and disbursements

In many legal transactions, it is common for a firm to ask a client to pay some money towards their profit costs (and expenses or 'disbursements') up front before any legal work is undertaken. This is often called 'money on account of costs and disbursements' or 'money on account'. This practice protects a firm by ensuring that the firm can minimise the use of business money to pay for disbursements, and it also serves as a good indication that the client will be able to pay their bill in due course.

Example ledger entries – payment of a bill

We will continue the case study of Amina Patel considered previously. We will now add the accounting entries to record the receipt of Amina's payment of £360 (to cover her reduced bill of £300 + £60 VAT), as shown in **Figure 5.3**. The entries relating to the payment of the bill are highlighted in italics.

Client ledger: Amina Patel (extract) Matter: Power of Attorney							
		Business account			Client account		
Date	Details	DR	CR	Bal	DR	CR	Bal
	Profit costs	400		400 DR			
	HMRC-VAT	80		480 DR			
	Profit costs (abatement)		100	380 DR			
	HMRC-VAT (abatement)		20	360 DR			
	Cash – payment of bill		*360*	–			

Cash sheet (extract)							
		Business account			Client account		
Date	Details	DR	CR	Bal	DR	CR	Bal
	Existing balances			XX			XX
	Amina Patel power of attorney – payment of bill	*360*		XX			XX

Figure 5.3: Ledger entries to record payment of a bill

> **Exam warning**
>
> Your understanding of the accounting entries required to record
> the payment of a client's bill may be tested in the SQE1 assessment.
> Remember that when a client pays their bill, the accounting entries are
> in the client ledger and the cash sheet. There are *no* entries in the profit
> costs and HMRC-VAT ledgers.

Money held on account of costs and disbursements

If a firm asks a client to send money on account of costs and unpaid
disbursements in a legal matter, the accounting entries must record the
receipt as client money, paid into the client account.

The relevant journal entries for a receipt of money on account of costs and
unpaid disbursements are therefore *CR client ledger client account* and *DR
cash sheet client account*.

Once a bill has been delivered, the firm can transfer the relevant sum from
the client account to the business account to clear the bill. This involves two
pairs of double entries and is recorded as a client to business cash transfer
(see **Chapter 6** for more details on cash transfers). The relevant journal
entries are:

1) *DR client ledger client account* and *CR cash sheet client account* (to
    transfer the sum out of the client account); and

2) *CR client ledger business account* and *DR cash sheet business account*
    (to transfer the sum into the business account).

You should memorise these accounting entries in case you are assessed on
this topic in the SQE1 assessment.

Example ledger entries – receipt of money on account of costs and disbursements

The following case study illustrates the accounting entries required to record
a receipt of money sent by the client on account of costs and disbursements
at the outset of a matter.

Rafael Diaz has instructed a firm to act for him in a conveyancing matter
relating to a house purchase. He is asked to send £300 on account of costs
and disbursements at the outset of the matter. The ledgers in **Figure 5.4**
show the entries made when he pays the money on account.

Client ledger: Rafael Diaz Matter: Purchase of 1 Brook Street, Rillcester							
		Business account			Client account		
Date	Details	DR	CR	Bal	DR	CR	Bal
	Cash – on account of costs and disbursements					300	300 CR

Cash sheet (extract)							
		Business account			Client account		
Date	Details	DR	CR	Bal	DR	CR	Bal
	Existing balances			XX			XX
	Rafael Diaz purchase of 1 Brook Street – on account of costs and disbursements			XX	300		XX

Figure 5.4: Ledger entries to record receipt of money on account of costs and disbursements

---

Revision tip

- If a law firm holds money on the *client account* in respect of fees and unpaid disbursements, this is still *client money* until a bill is submitted.
- When a bill has been submitted, the money to cover the fees and any paid disbursements will become *business money* and can be transferred into the *business account*.

Note: Money from the client account cannot be transferred to the business account in payment of a bill if it is intended for another purpose.

■ KEY POINT CHECKLIST

This chapter has covered the following key knowledge points. You can use these to structure your revision, ensuring you recall the key details for each point, as covered in this chapter.

- Law firms must keep a record of all bills that is readily accessible.

- When submitting a bill, a law firm will make ledger entries in the client ledger, the profit costs ledger and the HMRC-VAT ledger. There are *no entries in the cash sheet.* All the entries will be in the business account columns of the ledgers. The entries on the client ledger are debits and the entries on the profit costs and HMRC-VAT ledgers are credits.
- An abatement is a bill reduction. When recording an abatement, a law firm will make ledger entries in the same ledgers as when submitting a bill. However, the entries are reversed, that is, the entries on the client ledger are credits and the entries on the profit costs and HMRC-VAT ledgers are debits.
- When a client pays a bill, the firm will make ledger entries in the client ledger and the cash sheet. There are *no entries in the profit costs and HMRC-VAT ledgers.* All the entries will be in the *business account* columns of the ledgers. The entry on the client ledger is a credit and the entry on the cash sheet is a debit.
- Money paid on account of costs and unpaid disbursements is *client money* and must be paid into the *client account (not the business account)* until a bill is submitted.
- Once a bill is submitted, money held in the client account (in respect of fees and disbursements) can be transferred from the client account to the business account to clear the bill.
- The accounting entries for a receipt of money to pay a bill will be in the business account columns. The credit will be on the client ledger and the debit will be on the cash sheet.

■ KEY TERMS AND CONCEPTS

- profit costs (**page 81**)
- VAT (**page 81**)
- Her Majesty's Revenue and Customs (HMRC) (**page 82**)
- abatement (**page 84**)
- money on account of costs and disbursements (**page 87**)

■ SQE1-STYLE QUESTIONS

QUESTION 1

A firm of solicitors is acting on behalf of the administrators of an estate. They have just submitted their bill for £1,000 + VAT to the clients.

What accounting entries are required to record the submission of the bill?

A. Debit cash sheet business account with £1,000 for profit costs and £200 for VAT, credit profit costs ledger with £1,000 and credit Her Majesty's Revenue and Customs (HMRC)-VAT ledger with £200.

B. Debit cash sheet business account with £1,000 for profit costs and £200 for VAT, credit client ledger business account with £1,200.

C. Debit client ledger business account with £1,000 for profit costs and £200 for VAT, credit profit costs ledger with £1,000 and credit HMRC-VAT ledger with £200.

D. Credit client ledger business account with £1,000 for profit costs and £200 for VAT, debit profit costs ledger with £1,000 and debit HMRC-VAT ledger with £200.

E. Credit cash sheet client account with £1,000 for profit costs and £200 for VAT, debit profit costs ledger with £1,000 and debit HMRC-VAT ledger with £200.

QUESTION 2

A firm of solicitors has billed a client £600 + VAT for a conveyancing transaction. However, the client has asked for an abatement due to mistakes made by the firm which caused delays. The firm agrees to reduce the bill to £500 + VAT.

What accounting entries are required to record the reduction in the bill?

A. Credit client ledger business account with £100 for profit costs and £20 for VAT, debit profit costs ledger with £100 and debit Her Majesty's Revenue and Customs (HMRC)-VAT ledger with £20.

B. Credit client ledger business account with £500 and debit cash sheet business account with £100.

C. Credit client ledger business account with £500 for profit costs and £100 for VAT, debit profit costs ledger with £500 and debit HMRC-VAT ledger with £100.

D. Credit client ledger client account with £120 and debit cash sheet client account with £120.

E. Credit cash sheet business account with £500 profit costs and £100 VAT, debit profit costs ledger with £500 and HMRC-VAT ledger with £100.

QUESTION 3

A firm of solicitors has billed a client for drawing up their will. The client pays the bill in full by bank transfer.

What accounting entries are required to record the receipt of the client's payment to clear the bill?

A. Credit client ledger business account, debit profit costs ledger and debit Her Majesty's Revenue and Customs (HMRC)-VAT ledger.

B. Debit client ledger business account and credit cash sheet business account.

C. Debit cash sheet business account, credit profit costs ledger and credit HMRC-VAT ledger.

D. Credit client ledger business account and debit cash sheet business account.

E. Credit cash sheet business account, debit profit costs ledger and debit HMRC-VAT ledger.

QUESTION 4

A firm of solicitors has billed a client £300 + VAT for setting up a trust. There is currently £60 credit in the client ledger client account. The client sends a cheque for £300 towards payment of the bill.

Which of the following best explains which account the cheque should be paid into?

A. The cheque is client money and can be paid into the client account so it can be added to the credit balance of £60. The total amount can then be transferred into the business account to clear the bill.

B. The cheque is client money because the client has sent it. It should be paid into the client account.

C. The cheque is business money because it is received in payment of a bill. It should be paid into the business account.

D. The cheque is business money but should be paid into the client account because it is insufficient to cover the amount that the client has been billed.

E. The cheque is business money and should be paid into the business account so that it can be used to pay for future disbursements.

QUESTION 5

A client asks a law firm to draft a commercial tenancy agreement on her behalf. The client meets one of the solicitors to discuss the terms of the tenancy and asks for a quotation for costs and disbursements. The solicitor tells the client that it usually costs £700 (including disbursements, costs and VAT) for this type of tenancy. The client asks the solicitor for the relevant account details so that she can make an initial bank transfer of £400.

Which of the firm's bank accounts should the £400 be paid into?

A. The money should be paid into the firm's business bank account as it is intended to be used towards payment of the firm's profit costs and disbursements.

B. The money can be split so that the element relating to profit costs (and associated VAT) can be paid into the business bank account and the element relating to unpaid disbursements (and associated VAT) can be paid into the client bank account.

C. The money should be paid into the client bank account because the client has not yet paid the full £700 which has been quoted.

D. The firm can choose which bank account to pay the money into. By sending this money, the client has given the firm permission to choose the account that works best for them.

E. The money should be paid into the client bank account because it is on account of costs and unpaid disbursements. The firm has not yet sent a bill to the client or given her any written notification of costs.

■ ANSWERS TO QUESTIONS

Answers to 'What do you know already?' questions at the start of the chapter

1) True. Firms are required to keep a central record of all bills that is readily accessible (Rule 8.4).

2) The accounting entries (journal entries) required when submitting a bill are:
    -   DR client ledger (business account) with profit costs and CR profit costs ledger;
    -   DR client ledger (business account) with VAT and CR HMRC-VAT ledger with VAT.

3) True. There are no accounting entries required in the cash sheet because no money has been paid at this point. The accounting entries are recorded in the client, profit costs and HMRC-VAT ledgers respectively.

4) The correct answer was (c). The accounting entries required to record the reduction in a client's bill are: CR client ledger business account, DR profit costs ledger and DR HMRC-VAT ledger.

5) False. You cannot pay any money sent towards your professional fees into your business bank account until you have sent your client a bill or written notification of costs. Rule 2.1(d) provides that this is still client money until you have submitted your bill and therefore it must be paid into the client bank account.

Answers to end-of-chapter SQE1-style questions

Question 1:

The correct answer was C. This is because you must record the delivery of the bill in three ledgers (client, profit costs and HMRC-VAT). All entries will be in the *business account* columns because the bill reflects your charges for the legal services provided by your firm:

- debit client ledger business account (£1,000 entry for profit costs element and £200 entry for VAT element)
- credit profit costs ledger with £1,000
- credit HMRC-VAT ledger with £200 VAT.

Watch out – you *never make an entry in the cash sheet* when you submit a bill because the clients have not yet paid your firm any money. Therefore, options A, B and E are incorrect as they refer to entries in the cash sheet. Option D is incorrect because although the entries are in the correct ledgers and recorded in the business account columns, the *debits and credits are the wrong way around*. These ledger entries would be appropriate to record a bill abatement instead.

Question 2:

The correct answer was A. This is because you must record the reduction of the bill in the same three ledgers as when you submitted the bill (client, profit costs and HMRC-VAT). All entries will be in the *business account*, but *the debits and credits will be opposite to when you submitted the bill:*

- Credit client ledger business account (£100 entry for profit costs element and £20 entry for VAT element).
- Debit profit costs ledger with £100.
- Debit HMRC-VAT ledger with £20 VAT.

Watch out for the words used in the question – does it say that the bill is reduced *by* £500 + VAT or *to* £500 + VAT? In this question, the bill was reduced *to* £500 + VAT so the ledger entries reflect the *reduction* in the bill, that is, £100 + VAT. Therefore, you can discount options B, C and E because they refer to £500. There are *no entries in the cash sheet for an abatement.* Therefore, you can discount options B, D and E because they refer to the cash sheet.

Question 3:

The correct answer was D. When the client pays their bill, the money can go straight into the *business account* to clear the debt that the client owes you for the legal services that your firm has provided. The entries will be:

- Credit entry on client ledger to reflect that the client no longer owes a debt to your firm.
- Debit entry on cash sheet to reflect the receipt of the bill payment.

Watch out – you *never* make an entry in the profit costs and HMRC-VAT ledgers when you receive payment for a bill so you can discount options A, C and E. Option B has the debits and credits the wrong way around. Remember that when money is paid in, there is *always a debit entry in the cash sheet.*

Question 4:

The correct answer was C. As you have billed the client, the cheque is business money and must be paid into business account to cover part of the bill (the balance of £60 should be transferred from the client account to cover the rest of the bill if that is the intended purpose for which it is being held). Watch out that you do not automatically assume that all money sent by a client is client money (option B). Option E is incorrect because the purpose of the money is to cover part of the bill, not to cover future disbursements. The Rules require *business money* to be *kept separate* from *client money* so it is not appropriate for it to be paid into the client account (so options A and D are incorrect).

Question 5:

The correct answer was E. This is because the £400 payment is client money (although it was sent on account of costs and disbursements, it does not become business money until a bill, or written notification of costs, has been submitted to the client). You can therefore discount options A, B and D. Option C is correct in that the money must be paid into client account – however, the justification given for doing so is wrong. Once the firm bills the client, the money can be transferred into the business bank account. See **Chapter 6** for more information on transfers between accounts.

■ KEY RULES

The SRA Accounts Rules 2019 can be found on the SRA website.

The SQE1 Assessment Specification for Solicitors' Accounts does not require you to know individual Rule numbers, just the principles underpinning the Rules. However, you should familiarise yourself with the operation of:
• Rule 2.1(d)
• Rule 8.4

VAT and transfers

■ MAKE SURE YOU KNOW

This chapter is structured around elements of the SQE1 Assessment Specification relating to VAT, transfers and their respective accounting entries. It includes the following topics:

VAT

- VAT
- Disbursements not subject to VAT
- Disbursements subject to VAT:
  - Agency method
  - Principal method

Transfers

- Cash transfers:
  - Client to business transfer
  - Business to client transfer
  - Mixed receipts
- Inter-client transfers:
  - Transfers between clients
  - Transfers between matters

■ SQE ASSESSMENT ADVICE

As you work through this chapter, remember to pay particular attention in your revision to:

- how law firms account for VAT to HMRC using input tax and output tax
- the requirement for firms to keep and maintain accurate records in client ledgers
- how firms deal with disbursements that are not subject to VAT, including the related accounting entries
- how firms deal with disbursements that are subject to VAT, including the related accounting entries for dealing with VAT under either:
  - the agency method; or
  - the principal method

- the different types of transfers including cash transfers and inter-client transfers
- the accounting entries required to record such transfers.

■ WHAT DO YOU KNOW ALREADY?

Have a go at these questions before reading this chapter. If you find some difficult or cannot remember the answers, make a note to look more closely at that during your revision.

1) How does a firm account to HMRC for VAT?

    [VAT, page 97]

2) In which of the following examples of payments made by a firm would the principal method for dealing with VAT on disbursements be used?

    a) Payment of a court fee.

    b) Payment of an invoice which is in the client's name.

    c) Payment of an invoice which is in the firm's name.

    [Disbursements subject to VAT, page 102]

3) What are the journal entries for payment of a disbursement subject to VAT using the agency method?

    [Agency method – client's name on invoice, page 102]

4) True or false? An inter-client transfer involves movement of money between the client bank account and the business bank account.

    [Transfers, page 110]

5) What are the journal entries for an inter-client transfer where a client asks that money is transferred between two matters in which the firm is acting for them?

    [Inter-client transfers, page 116]

VAT

We have already considered VAT on profit costs in **Chapter 5**. Now we will look at how VAT affects law firms more broadly, together with a focus on how firms deal with VAT on expenses and disbursements.

All businesses *must* be registered for VAT if their turnover exceeds the VAT registration threshold (currently £85,000 per year) but can *choose* to be registered for VAT if their turnover falls below this threshold. Almost all law firms are VAT registered.

VAT is a consumer tax: the ultimate burden of the tax falls on the final consumer because they are not VAT registered. However, VAT registered businesses offset any VAT that they pay (**input tax**) against any VAT that they charge (**output tax**) so do not bear the burden of the tax. They must complete a **VAT return** (usually online) every quarter to pay HMRC the balance of VAT owing (output tax less input tax). They must also issue their customers or clients with VAT invoices so that any who are VAT registered can complete their own VAT returns.

A law firm may have clients who are registered for VAT (eg commercial property companies) and clients who are not registered for VAT (eg family members acting as personal representatives in a probate matter).

Key term: input tax

A firm pays VAT on most goods or services that it buys. This includes VAT on goods or services needed to run its own business, for example computing equipment and office cleaning services; or VAT on services that it pays for on behalf of clients, for example experts' fees. VAT paid on goods or services coming *into* the firm is called *input tax.*

Key term: output tax

A firm charges VAT on the legal services it supplies to clients. This includes VAT on its own professional fees (profit costs) but also on services supplied to the firm on behalf of clients which the firm recharges the clients for. VAT charged on services going *out* of the firm is called *output tax.*

Key term: VAT return

A VAT return is a form completed by VAT-registered businesses every three months, usually online, detailing their input tax and output tax for that period. The firm must submit the form to HMRC.

Practice example 6.1 illustrates how this topic might be assessed in the SQE1 assessment.

Practice example 6.1

A firm completes its VAT return for the most recent VAT quarterly accounting period. The firm checks its HMRC-VAT ledger. During the relevant three months, it has charged £235,000 *output tax* on the legal services it has supplied to clients. During the same period, it has paid £100,000 *input tax* on goods and supplies that it has bought.

How much VAT must the firm pay to HMRC for this quarter?

The firm must pay £135,000 VAT to HMRC (£235,000 *output tax* less £100,000 *input tax*).

Most goods and services, *including legal services,* are taxed at the standard VAT rate of 20%. However, some goods and supplies are exempt from VAT, for example health services and most supplies of land. Some goods and supplies are zero-rated (taxed at 0%) or taxed at 5%.

As HMRC expects firms to account for VAT on all legal services that they provide, firms must remember to include VAT on all quotations that they give to clients.

EXPENSES AND DISBURSEMENTS

When firms provide legal services, they may pay expenses on behalf of their clients to progress the legal matters involved. For example, a firm acting in a probate matter may pay expenses such as probate court fees or valuation fees. The firm must charge clients VAT on some expenses but not others.

Firms often refer to all expenses as disbursements. However, strictly speaking only some of them will qualify as *'disbursements for VAT purposes'* (as defined by HRMC). Firms do not have to charge their clients VAT on 'disbursements for VAT purposes'. **Table 6.1** includes more details on different types of disbursements and how they are treated for VAT purposes.

Table 6.1: Different types of disbursements and how they are treated for VAT purposes

	Expenses recognised as 'disbursements for VAT purposes'	Expenses *not* recognised as 'disbursements for VAT purposes'*	
Type of expense	Expenses that are deemed to be separate from the legal services provided by the firm, ie the firm merely arranges for the supply of the third-party service to the client	Expenses that are treated as part of the firm's overheads in providing legal services to clients	Expenses that are deemed to be integral to the legal services provided by the firm, eg where the firm provides legal advice on a service supplied by a third party
Examples of expenses	• Stamp Duty Land Tax • Land Registry registration fee • Probate fees • Court fees	• Postage • Travel expenses • Photocopying • Printing	• Some conveyancing searches • Experts' fees

Table 6.1: (continued)

	Expenses recognised as 'disbursements for VAT purposes'	Expenses *not* recognised as 'disbursements for VAT purposes'*	
How expenses are treated on the firm's invoice to the client	The expense is shown separately on the firm's invoice to the client (without VAT)	The expenses are normally included in the profit costs (+ VAT) element of the firm's invoice so are not listed separately	The expense + VAT is normally shown separately on the firm's invoice to the client
Is VAT charged to the client?	No	Yes	Yes

*Following recent case law, there is confusion over whether certain expenses can still be considered as 'disbursements for VAT purposes'. The Law Society has issued guidance to firms on, for example, conveyancing searches, but has also requested further clarification from HMRC and the courts on this matter.

Disbursements not subject to VAT

Some disbursements are not subject to VAT, so the firm *does not have to charge clients VAT* on them.

If a firm pays for a disbursement that is not subject to VAT on behalf of a client, then the firm will not pay VAT when paying for the disbursement initially, or charge VAT on the disbursement when billing the client. If the client has sufficient funds available in the client account, this will be used to pay for the disbursement. If not, the disbursement can be paid from the business account. In the SQE1 assessment you may be asked to identify the accounting entries required to record payment of a disbursement not subject to VAT. The relevant accounting entries (journal entries) are shown in **Table 6.2**.

Table 6.2: Accounting entries required to record payment of a disbursement not subject to VAT

If paid from the *client* account (where sufficient funds are available):	If paid from the *business* account (if there are insufficient funds in the client account):
• DR client ledger *client* account • CR cash sheet *client* account	• DR client ledger *business* account • CR cash sheet *business* account

The following case study illustrates the accounting entries for such a disbursement in the firm's ledgers.

Example of ledger entries for payment of disbursements not subject to VAT

A firm is instructed by Eva Wilton who is purchasing a property as a cash buyer. The firm must pay a Land Registry registration fee of £150 (a disbursement not subject to VAT) to register the transfer of the property to Eva. Eva has already paid the firm sufficient money (held in the client account) to complete the purchase, including the costs of the registration fee. Therefore, this fee can be paid from the client account. The ledger entries are shown in **Figure 6.1** in the client ledger and cash sheet.

Client ledger: Eva Wilton (extract) Matter: Purchase of 8 Coldharbour Street							
		Business account			Client account		
Date	Details	DR	CR	Bal	DR	CR	Bal
	Existing balances			XX			XX CR
	Cash – Land Registry registration fee			XX	150		XX CR

Cash sheet (extract)							
		Business account			Client account		
Date	Details	DR	CR	Bal	DR	CR	Bal
	Existing balances			XX			XX DR
	Eva Wilton purchase of 8 Coldharbour Street – Land Registry registration fee			XX		150	XX DR

Figure 6.1: Ledger entries to record payment of a disbursement not subject to VAT

If Eva did not have sufficient funds in the *client account*, the payment could be made from the *business account* initially, and then claimed back from her in due course.

Disbursements subject to VAT

Many disbursements paid by firms on behalf of clients are subject to VAT, that is, the third party charges VAT when supplying the goods or service. For example, a firm instructs a property surveyor to value the deceased's property for probate purposes. The property surveyor will usually charge VAT on their fee. The firm will pass on the charge to the client, including the VAT element, but will not charge any additional VAT.

As **Table 6.3** indicates, there are two ways of doing this, depending on whose name is on the third party's invoice.

Table 6.3: Agency or principal method of dealing with VAT

Client's name on invoice	Use the **agency method***
Firm's name on invoice	Use the **principal method**

*Counsel's fees may also be accounted for using the agency method as an exception to the general principle (see **Counsel's fees, page 109**).

Key term: agency method

Sometimes the law firm acts as *agent* in arranging for a third party to supply services to the client and in then paying for the services on behalf of the client, that is, the services are supplied to the client rather than the firm and the firm just acts as intermediary. The third party's invoice is therefore issued to the client (rather than the firm) and so it is the client who is liable for the VAT. Therefore, there is no need for the firm to make any entries on its HMRC-VAT ledger.

Key term: principal method

Sometimes the law firm acts as *principal* when ordering services from a supplier on behalf of the client, that is, the services are supplied to the firm rather than the client. The firm is therefore liable for the VAT and will pass on the charges for the supplier's services to the client. Both input tax (paid by the firm to the supplier) and output tax (charged to the client by the firm) must be recorded in the firm's HMRC-VAT ledger.

It is important that a firm uses the agency and principal methods correctly when accounting for the payment of disbursements subject to VAT, so that both the firm and the client (if VAT registered and paying for the service in the course of their business) are able to account to HMRC properly on their respective VAT returns.

Agency method – client's name on invoice

If a third party supplies goods or services required in the course of a legal matter, it may invoice the client direct but send the invoice to the law firm to pay it on the client's behalf. In this situation, the name of the client will be on the invoice, that is, the client is directly liable to the third party for the payment. The firm merely acts as an *agent* for the client when making the payment on their behalf. As the VAT element of the payment is the responsibility of the client *not* the firm, there is no need to make any ledger entries in the firm's HMRC-VAT ledger.

If the client is VAT registered and the goods or services relate to the client's business, they may ask the firm to send them the original VAT invoice from the third party. The client will then use the invoice for their own VAT records and VAT return calculations.

When using the agency method, it is usual to use client money to pay the third party. However, if there are insufficient funds available in the client account, the payment can be made from the business account. In either situation, there is only one payment made which encompasses both the *fee* for the service or goods *plus the associated VAT*. The VAT element should *not* be accounted for separately.

The accounting entries (journal entries) for payment of a *disbursement subject to VAT* using the *agency method* are shown in **Table 6.4**.

Table 6.4: Journal entries to record payment of a disbursement subject to VAT using the agency method

If paid from the *client* account (where sufficient funds are available):	If paid from the *business* account (where sufficient funds are *not* available in the client account):
• DR client ledger *client* account • CR cash sheet *client* account	• DR client ledger *business* account • CR cash sheet *business* account

You should memorise these accounting entries so that you are able to identify the correct answer if required to do so in an SQE1 assessment question.

Exam warning

When identifying the correct answer on an SQE1 assessment question on this topic, remember that if the invoice is in the *client's* name, the *agency method* must be used. This means that:
- the accounting entries for paying the disbursement are *VAT-inclusive* (ie they include both the fee + VAT as one sum)
- the accounting entries will be in the client ledger and the cash sheet. *No entries* are made in the HMRC-VAT ledger as the *VAT liability lies with the client not the firm.*

Example ledger entries – agency method
It may help you to memorise the appropriate accounting entries if you are able to visualise how they appear on the firm's ledgers. Therefore, the following case study illustrates the ledger entries for a disbursement subject to VAT using the agency method.

A firm acts for the executors of Gupta Patel deceased. The solicitor instructs a local property surveyor, Ella Rains, to provide a probate valuation of Gupta's home. Ella's invoice for £1,000 + VAT is in the name of the executors, although she sends it to the firm to be paid on the clients' behalf. There are sufficient funds in the client account to pay the invoice. The invoice is paid on 1st January.

The ledger entries are shown in **Figure 6.2**. You will note that there is one entry in each ledger for the VAT-inclusive amount of £1,200 (£1,000 fee + £200 VAT).

Client ledger: Executors of Gupta Patel deceased (extract) Matter: Probate							
		Business account			Client account		
Date	Details	DR	CR	Bal	DR	CR	Bal
	Existing balances			–			50,000 CR
1 Jan	Cash – E Rains property valuation (VAT included)			–	1,200		48,800 CR

Cash sheet (extract)							
		Business account			Client account		
Date	Details	DR	CR	Bal	DR	CR	Bal
	Existing balances			XX			XX
1 Jan	Executors of Gupta Patel deceased – E Rains property valuation			XX		1,200	XX

Figure 6.2: Ledger entries to record payment of a disbursement subject to VAT using the agency method

Practice example 6.2 illustrates how you might be assessed on accounting entries for a disbursement subject to VAT using the agency method in the SQE1 assessment.

Practice example 6.2

A solicitor acts for the executors in a probate matter. The solicitor receives an invoice for £100 + VAT from an antiques specialist for valuing some of the assets that belonged to the deceased. The invoice is made out in the name of the executors. The client ledger shows a credit balance of £100 in the client account.

What accounting entries are required to record the payment of this invoice?

As the invoice is in the *clients' name*, the solicitor must use the *agency method*. She must therefore record the payment of £120 as a VAT-inclusive sum (ie £100 fee + £20 VAT). The client has *insufficient funds available to pay this sum from the client account*, so it must be paid from *the business account* instead. The accounting entries (journal entries) would therefore be:

DR £120 on client ledger business account and CR £120 on cash sheet business account.

Principal method – firm's name on invoice

If a third party supplies goods or services to a law firm (rather than the firm's client), the invoice will be made out in the name of the firm (rather than the client). This means that the firm must use the *principal method* when accounting for the payment of this disbursement. The firm is responsible for paying the VAT on the supply, even though the goods or services are connected with a legal matter in which they are acting for a specific client. The firm will then recharge the fee and the associated VAT to the client when they deliver a bill to them. In this situation, the firm pays for the goods or services as *principal* (rather than as agent) and therefore the ledger entries involve two stages:

1) The third party supplies the goods or services to the firm in exchange for payment.
2) The firm recharges the supply to the client when they bill them, usually at the same time as billing for their profit costs.*

* Note: If there are sufficient funds in the client account, the firm may then do a cash transfer from the client account to the business account to cover the bill (see **Cash transfers, page 111**). Alternatively, the client may make a direct payment which can be received straight into the business account (see **Chapter 5, Payment of a bill, page 86**).

The accounting entries (journal entries) for the two stages involved in paying a *disbursement subject to VAT* using the *principal method* are shown in **Table 6.5** and **Table 6.6**.

Table 6.5: Stage 1 – firm pays disbursement + VAT

Two pairs of double entries are required:		
1.	Disbursement	DR client ledger business account CR cash sheet business account
2.	VAT	DR HMRC-VAT ledger* CR cash sheet business account

Input tax.

Table 6.6: Stage 2 – firm recharges disbursement to client when billing for profit costs

Two pairs of double entries are required:		
1.	Profit costs	DR client ledger business account CR profit costs ledger
2.	VAT (on both profit costs and disbursement)	DR client ledger business account CR HMRC-VAT ledger*

Output tax.

You should memorise these accounting entries. Although an SQE1 assessment question may test your understanding of this type of transaction as a whole, it may also assess you on just one element or stage of the transaction.

Exam warning

When identifying the correct answer on an SQE1 assessment question on this topic, remember that:

- If the third party's invoice is in the firm's name, you *must* use the *principal method*.
- When using the *principal method*, the disbursement *must* be paid from the *business account*.
- The entry on the client ledger is for a *VAT-exclusive sum*.
- When the firm bills the client, it will charge the client VAT on the disbursement (together with any VAT owing on profit costs).
- The firm must record entries in their HMRC-VAT ledger for both:
  - the *input tax* that they pay to the third party (when they pay the disbursement); and
  - the *output tax* that they recharge to the client (when they bill the client).

Example ledger entries – principal method

You may find it easier to understand the more complex series of accounting entries required for the principal method if you can visualise the entries on the ledgers for the different stages. We will therefore continue the case study concerning Gupta Patel deceased to illustrate this.

The firm instructs an accounting firm, MM Accountants LLP, to value Gupta Patel's business at the date of his death as part of the valuation of his estate. MM Accountants LLP send an invoice for their services for £2000 + VAT. The firm's name is on the invoice so the principal method of accounting for VAT must be used. The firm pays the bill on 1st February.

On 1st March, the firm bills the executors for £5,000 profit costs + VAT. At the time of billing, the firm also recharges the disbursement + VAT (for the probate valuation of Gupta's business).

The ledgers in **Figure 6.3** illustrate the accounting entries required to record payment of a disbursement using the principal method. The entries for each of the two stages are shaded differently so that it is easier to identify the respective ledger entries.

Stage 1	1 Feb	Firm pays accountant's fee + VAT (£2,000 + £400 VAT) from the *business account* as *principal*. NB only the fee (without the VAT) is recorded in the DR column of the client ledger on 1 Feb, with a note in the details column to include VAT on the fee when billing the client
Stage 2	1 March	Firm bills client for profit costs (£5,000) and VAT on both profit costs and accountant's fee (£1,000 VAT on profit costs + £400 VAT on fee = £1,400)

Client ledger: Executors of Gupta Patel deceased (extract)
Matter: Probate

Date	Details	Business account			Client account		
		DR	CR	Bal	DR	CR	Bal
	Existing balances			–			50,000 CR
1 Jan	Cash – E Rains property valuation (VAT included)			–	1,200		48,800 CR
1 Feb	Cash – MM Accountants LLP *(NB £400 VAT to be collected)*	2,000		2,000 DR			48,800 CR
1 Mar	Profit costs	5,000		7,000 DR			48,800 CR
1 Mar	HMRC-VAT (£1,000 VAT on profit costs + £400 VAT on accountant's fee)	1,400		8,400 DR			48,800 CR

Figure 6.3: Ledger entries to record payment of a disbursement using the principal method

HMRC-VAT ledger (extract)				
		Business account		
Date	Details	DR	CR	Bal
	Existing balances			XX
1 Feb	Executors of Gupta Patel deceased – VAT on MM Accountants LLP report	400*		XX
1 Mar	Executors of Gupta Patel deceased – VAT on profit costs and disbursements		1,400**	XX

*Input tax.
**Output tax.

Cash sheet (extract)							
		Business account			Client account		
Date	Details	DR	CR	Bal	DR	CR	Bal
	Existing balances			XX			XX CR
1 Jan	Executors of Gupta Patel deceased – E Rains property valuation (VAT included)			XX		1,200	XX CR
1 Feb	Executors of Gupta Patel deceased – MM Accountants LLP report		2,000	XX			XX CR
1 Feb	HMRC-VAT – executors of Gupta Patel deceased, VAT on MM Accountants LLP report		400	XX			XX CR

Figure 6.3: (continued)

Profit costs ledger (extract)				
		Business account		
Date	Details	DR	CR	Bal
	Existing balances			XX
1 Mar	Executors of Gupta Patel deceased		5,000	XX

Figure 6.3: (continued)

Revision tip

Remember that when you are using the *principal method*:
- *All* ledger entries are in the *business account* columns at both stages 1 and 2.
- There are *no entries* in the *cash sheet* at stage 2 because the client has not yet paid for the profit costs and disbursements included in the bill.

Practice example 6.3 illustrates how you might be assessed on accounting entries for a disbursement subject to VAT using the *principal method* in the SQE1 assessment.

Practice example 6.3

A solicitor acts for a client in a conveyancing matter and receives an invoice from a surveyor for a property valuation. The invoice is for £1,500 + VAT and is in the law firm's name.

How should the firm deal with this invoice?

As the invoice is in the name of the firm, the *principal method* of accounting must be used. Payment must be made from the business bank account and the firm must pay VAT initially. When the firm bills the client, it will pass on the charge for the survey and recharge the client for the associated VAT.

Counsel's fees

A firm may instruct counsel (eg a barrister) on behalf of their client. Counsel will invoice the firm, using the firm's name. As such, you would expect the VAT on counsel's fees to be dealt with using the principal method.

However, for many years, HMRC has granted an extra-statutory concession (an exception to the general principle) to law firms so that they can choose to deal with counsel's fees using the agency method. To use the agency method, they should substitute the client's name for the firm's name on the invoice. The invoice must then be sent to the client for their own VAT records. However, this concession is currently under review and may be removed.

Revision tip

Check whose name the invoice is in. If it is in the *firm name*, you must use the *principal method* and make the payment from the *business account*. If it is in the *client's name*, you must use the *agency method* and make the payment from the *client account* (if there are sufficient client funds available for this purpose). If not, make the payment from the *business account*. See **Table 6.7** by way of a reminder.

Table 6.7: Summary of the agency and principal methods of dealing with VAT

Agency method	Principal method
Client's name on invoice (or counsel fees if HMRC concession used)	Firm's name on invoice
Pay from the client account if sufficient funds; if not, pay from the business account	*Always* pay from the business account
Ledger entries are for VAT-*inclusive* sum	Ledger entries (on the client ledger) are for VAT-*exclusive* sum

TRANSFERS

Firms often need to make transfers as part of their standard accounting practices. This section will discuss **cash transfers** and **inter-client transfers**.

Key term: cash transfer

A cash transfer is a transfer of money from the client bank account to the business bank account or vice versa. As a cash transfer involves money moving from one bank account to another, the necessary ledger entries will be recorded not only in the *client ledger*, but also in the *cash sheet*.

Key term: inter-client transfer

An inter-client transfer may involve either:
- a transfer between different clients (eg from client A to client B); or
- a transfer between different matters for the same client (eg client A-*matter A* to client A-*matter B* – this is sometimes called an inter-matter or intra-matter transfer).

Either way, the transfer will involve client money that remains in the client bank account but is simply switched from one client (or matter) to another. The necessary ledger entries will therefore be recorded in *two separate client ledgers.* There will be *no entries on the cash sheet* as money is not being transferred into or out of the client account.

Cash transfers

Rule 4.1 of the SRA Accounts Rules ('the Rules' – see **Chapter 1**) requires firms to keep 'client money separate from money belonging to the authorised body'. Firms comply with this Rule by holding *client* money in a *client bank account* and *business* money in a *business bank account* (see **Chapter 1**). However, sometimes it is necessary to make cash transfers that move money between the business and client bank accounts. Each cash transfer relates to one client and one matter.

Revision tip

Accounting entries for *cash transfers* are made in the *client ledger* and in the *cash sheet*.

Two pairs of ledger entries are required for each transfer:
1) Transfer *out* of one bank account.
2) Transfer *into* the other bank account.

Client to business cash transfer

One of the most common examples of a *client to business cash transfer* is a transfer of profit costs (and disbursements) following submission of a bill. In **Chapter 5**, we saw that once a bill has been submitted, *client money* held in the *client account* may become *business money* (if it is not intended for another purpose) and can therefore be transferred into the *business account* (see **Chapter 5, Payment of a bill, page 86**).

Rule 4.3 allows such a transfer to be made if:
• some or all the money in the client account is intended to cover the firm's costs
• a bill has been submitted to the client
• the transfer is for the specific sum billed.

The accounting entries (journal entries) for a *client to business cash transfer* require two pairs of double entries, for example to clear money owed to the firm following submission of a bill:
1) *Transfer out* of client account – DR client ledger client account and CR cash sheet client account.
2) *Transfer into* business account – CR client ledger business account and DR cash sheet business account.

Some firms make these entries over two lines of their ledgers with the '*transfer out*' on one line and the '*transfer in*' on the line below. However, many firms make these entries on the same line of the ledgers, as illustrated in **Figure 6.4**.

You should memorise these accounting entries so that you are able to recognise the correct answer on an SQE1 assessment question on this topic.

Example ledger entries – client to business cash transfer

Continuing the case study concerning Gupta Patel's probate, you will recall that your firm submitted a bill to Gupta's executors for profit costs and disbursements and associated VAT on 1st March. The bill total is £8,400. The executors approve the estate accounts on 5th March. As there is a sufficient credit balance in the client account, the firm records a *client to business cash transfer* on 5th March to transfer the funds to clear the bill. The balance remaining in the client account can then be distributed to the beneficiaries in accordance with the terms of Gupta's will.

The ledger entries for the *client to business cash transfer* are shown in **Figure 6.4**.

5 March	Transfer of £8,400 from client account to business account to cover monies owing to the firm

Client ledger: Executors of Gupta Patel deceased (extract)
Matter: Probate

Date	Details	Business account			Client account		
		DR	CR	Bal	DR	CR	Bal
	Existing balances			–			50,000 CR
1 Jan	Cash – E Rains property valuation (VAT included)			–	1,200		48,800 CR
1 Feb	Cash – MM Accountants LLP (NB £400 VAT to be collected)	2,000		2,000 DR			48,800 CR
1 Mar	Profit costs	5,000		7,000 DR			48,800 CR
1 Mar	HMRC–VAT (£1,000 VAT on profit costs + £400 VAT on accountant's fee)	1,400		8,400 DR			48,800 CR
5 Mar	Cash – transfer from client to business account		8,400**	–	8,400*		40,400 CR

Figure 6.4: Ledger entries to record a client to business cash transfer

Cash sheet (extract)							
		Business account			Client account		
Date	Details	DR	CR	Bal	DR	CR	Bal
	Existing balances			XX			XX CR
1 Jan	Executors of Gupta Patel deceased – E Rains property valuation (VAT included)			XX		1,200	XX CR
1 Feb	Executors of Gupta Patel deceased – MM Accountants LLP report		2,000	XX			XX CR
1 Feb	HMRC-VAT – executors of Gupta Patel deceased, VAT on MM Accountants LLP report		400	XX			XX CR
1 Mar	Executors of Gupta Patel deceased – transfer client to business account of profit costs and disbursements	8,400**		XX		8,400*	XX CR

*Transfer *out of client account.*
**Transfer *into business account.*

Figure 6.4: (continued)

Business to client cash transfer

Sometimes a cash transfer is made from the business account to the client account. One example is when a client is paid a sum in lieu of interest. This has already been discussed in **Chapter 4, Step two – transferring a sum in lieu of interest from the business account to the client account, page 61.** Another example may occur where there has been a breach of the Rules such that client money has been improperly withheld from the client account or withdrawn from the client account in error. Under Rule 6.1, the firm must replace the client money immediately, and if there is no other alternative, they must transfer business money to do so using a *business to client cash transfer* (see **Chapter 3** for more details on how to correct a breach of the Rules).

The accounting entries (journal entries) for a *business to client cash transfer* require two pairs of double entries, for example to transfer a sum in lieu of interest or to correct a breach of the Rules:

1) *Transfer out* of the business account – DR client ledger business account and CR cash sheet business account.

2) *Transfer into* the client account – CR client ledger client account and DR cash sheet client account.

As for a client to cash transfer, these pairs of double entries can be made on either the same line of the client ledger and cash sheet, or over two lines (*'transfer out'* on one line and *'transfer in'* on the line below).

You should memorise these accounting entries so that you are able to recognise the correct answer on an SQE1 assessment question on this topic.

Mixed receipts

In some instances, a firm may receive a payment that is a mixture of *client money* and *business money*. This is called a *mixed receipt* (or *mixed payment*). Mixed receipts can be received either by bank transfer or by cheque, although payment by cheque is far less common nowadays.

If a mixed receipt is paid by bank transfer, the whole amount will be paid into one account before the element belonging to the other account is transferred. Rule 4.2 requires mixed receipts to be 'allocated promptly' to the correct account.

Firms have their own policies on how mixed receipts are dealt with. It is generally advisable to pay the mixed receipt into the *client account* first and then to transfer the *business money* element into the *business account*. This will be a straightforward *client to business cash transfer* and the ledger entries will reflect this.

However, the Rules also permit the mixed receipt to be paid into the *business account* first and then the *client money* element to be transferred into the *client account*. This would be a *business to client cash transfer* and the ledger entries would reflect this.

If a mixed receipt is paid by cheque, it is usual to pay the cheque into the client account and then to transfer the business money element into the business account. However, under the Rules, it is also permissible to pay it all into the business account and then to transfer the client money element into the client account. A third alternative is for the bank to split the cheque and pay the client money element straight into the client account and the business money element straight into the business account. Banks are not generally keen to split cheques, so this does not happen often.

Example ledger entries – mixed receipts

A firm acts for a client, Townland Properties Ltd, in an ongoing commercial property transaction. The firm sends an interim bill to the client for £10,000 to cover profit costs and disbursements to date (including any related VAT). The client makes a payment of £15,000 to cover the interim bill of £10,000 (*business money*) plus £5,000 towards future costs and disbursements (*client money*). This is a *mixed receipt*. The firm's policy is to pay all mixed receipts into the client account first before transferring the business money element into the business account.

The relevant accounting entries are illustrated in the ledgers in **Figure 6.5**.

Practice example 6.4 illustrates how an SQE1 assessment might test your understanding of mixed receipts.

Practice example 6.4
A client makes a payment of £1,000 to a firm by bank transfer. This sum represents a payment of £500 + VAT to cover billed profit costs. The rest of the funds are to be held on account of future costs and disbursements.
How should the firm deal with this payment?
This is a mixed receipt of £600 business money (£500 profit costs + £100 VAT, for which the client has already been billed) and £400 client money to be held on account of future costs and disbursements. It is best for the whole sum to be paid into the client account and then for the £600 business money element to be transferred promptly to the business account.

Client ledger: Townland Properties Ltd (extract) Matter: Grey Wharf 51 (purchase)							
		Business account			Client account		
Date	Details	DR	CR	Bal	DR	CR	Bal
	Existing balances			10,000 DR			XX CR
	Cash – payment of interim bill			10,000 DR		15,000	XX CR
	Cash – transfer from client to business account		10,000	–	10,000		XX CR

Figure 6.5: Ledger entries to record a mixed receipt

Cash sheet (extract)							
		Business account			Client account		
Date	Details	DR	CR	Bal	DR	CR	Bal
	Existing balances			XX			XX
	Townland Properties Ltd: Grey Wharf 51 – payment of interim bill			XX	15,000		XX
	Townland Properties Ltd Grey Wharf 51 – transfer from client to business account	10,000		XX		10,000	XX

Figure 6.5: (continued)

Inter-client transfers

An inter-client transfer may involve the transfer of client money from one client to another, or from one matter to another for the same client. In either case, there is no change in the balance of client money held in the firm's general client account. It is simply that some of the money in the account has been allocated differently, either to a different client, or to a different matter.

Revision tip

The accounting entries for an inter-client transfer involve *two client ledgers*, either for different clients, or for different matters for the same client. The *cash ledger* is not involved.

It may help you to imagine that in the general client account, there are different chunks of money belonging to the different clients of the firm. In an inter-client transfer, the relevant chunk of money does not leave the client account but is simply re-labelled as belonging to a different client.

Inter-client transfer between clients

In some situations, a client may instruct a firm to transfer *client money* from themselves to another client.

The accounting entries (journal entries) required to record an *inter-client transfer between clients* are straightforward – DR client A ledger client account and CR client B ledger client account. You should memorise these accounting entries so that you can identify the appropriate answer in an SQE1 assessment question on this topic. You may find it helpful to visualise the accounting entries in the firm's ledgers, so a case study illustrating this transaction is included in the next section.

Example ledger entries – inter-client transfer between clients

A firm acts for Salman Hussain in the sale of his sole trader business premises on his retirement. The firm also acts for his son, Bilal, who is buying his first home. Salman instructs you to transfer £10,000 from the net proceeds of sale of the business premises to Bilal, so that Bilal can use it towards the deposit on the house that he is buying.

The accounting entries are illustrated in the ledgers in **Figure 6.6**.

Client ledger: Salman Hussain (extract) Matter: Sale of Boone Buildings								
		Business account			**Client account**			
Date	Details	DR	CR	Bal	DR	CR	Bal
	Existing balances			XX			XX CR
	Bilal Hussain purchase of 12 Top Street – transfer towards deposit			XX	10,000		XX CR

Client ledger: Bilal Hussain (extract) Matter: Purchase of 12 Top Street								
		Business account			**Client account**			
Date	Details	DR	CR	Bal	DR	CR	Bal
	Existing balances			XX			XX CR
	Salman Hussain sale of Boone Buildings – transfer towards deposit			XX		10,000	XX CR

Figure 6.6: Ledger entries to record an inter-client transfer between two clients

Inter-client transfer between matters

If a firm acts for a client in two or more different matters at the same time, the client may sometimes instruct the firm to transfer *client money* from one matter to another.

The accounting entries (journal entries) required to record an inter-client transfer between two matters are straightforward – DR client ledger (matter A) client account and CR client ledger (matter B) client account. You should memorise these accounting entries so that you can identify the appropriate answer in an SQE1 assessment question on this topic. You may find it helpful to visualise the accounting entries in the firm's ledgers, so a case study illustrating this transaction is included in the next section.

> ### Exam warning
>
> If an SQE1 assessment question relates to the accounting entries required for an inter-client transfer, remember that there will be *no* entry on the cash sheet. Both ledger entries must be on the client ledgers.

Example ledger entries – inter-client transfer between matters

A firm acts for Salman Hussain in the sale of his business premises. However, he has also asked the firm to draft a will for him as a separate matter. He instructs the firm to transfer £600 from the net proceeds of sale in readiness to cover the costs of drafting the will in due course. This will involve an inter-client transfer from the sale ledger to the will drafting ledger as illustrated in the ledgers in **Figure 6.7**.

Client ledger: Salman Hussain (extract) Matter: Sale of Boone Buildings							
		Business account			Client account		
Date	Details	DR	CR	Bal	DR	CR	Bal
	Existing balances			XX			XX CR
	Salman Hussain will – transfer on account of costs			XX	600		XX CR

Figure 6.7: Ledger entries to record an inter-client transfer between two matters for the same client

Client ledger: Salman Hussain (extract) Matter: Will							
		Business account			Client account		
Date	Details	DR	CR	Bal	DR	CR	Bal
	Salman Hussain sale of Boone Buildings – transfer on account of costs			–		600	600 CR

Figure 6.7: (continued)

■ KEY POINT CHECKLIST

This chapter has covered the following key knowledge points. You can use these to structure your revision around, making sure to recall the key details for each point, as covered in this chapter.

- Most law firms are VAT registered and will account for VAT quarterly (output tax – input tax).
- Disbursements not subject to VAT can be paid from the client account if there are funds available, or from the business account if not.
- There are two ways of accounting for VAT on disbursements subject to VAT depending on whose name is on the invoice.
- Invoices in the name of the client (and sometimes counsel's fees) are dealt with using the *agency method*, and invoices in the name of the firm are dealt with using the *principal method*.
- Payments using the *agency method* can be from the client account if there are sufficient funds available for that purpose, or from the business account if not.
- Payments using the *principal method* must always be from the business account. Two stages are involved in this type of transaction: first, the firm must pay the disbursement as principal; and second, the firm must recharge the client for the disbursement and any associated VAT when they submit their next bill.
- *Cash transfers* can be made from the *client to the business account* or from the *business to the client account*. Two pairs of ledger entries are required: first to withdraw the money from one account; and second, to pay the money into the other account.
- *Inter-client transfers* are transfers between clients, or between matters. Accounting entries are required on the *two client ledgers*, but *not on the cash sheet* as the money stays in the general client account.

■ KEY TERMS AND CONCEPTS

- input tax (**page 98**)
- output tax (**page 98**)
- VAT return (**page 98**)
- agency method (**page 102**)
- principal method (**page 102**)
- cash transfer (**page 110**)
- inter-client transfer (**page 110**)

■ SQE1-STYLE QUESTIONS

QUESTION 1

A law firm completes its quarterly VAT return. During the relevant period, the firm has charged its clients profit costs of £775,000 + VAT for its legal services. During the same period, the firm has paid £175,000 + VAT to third parties for goods and services supplied to the firm.

Which of the following options best explains how the firm should account to Her Majesty's Revenue and Customs (HMRC) for VAT relating to this period?

A. £775,000 output tax less £175,000 input tax = £600,000 paid to HMRC.

B. £175,000 output tax less £775,000 input tax = £600,000 owed by HMRC to the firm.

C. £155,000 output tax less £35,000 input tax = £120,000 paid to HMRC.

D. £155,000 input tax less £35,000 output tax = £120,000 paid to HMRC.

E. £35,000 input tax less £155,000 output tax = £120,000 owed by HMRC to the firm.

QUESTION 2

A firm pays for a surveyor's valuation fee subject to VAT on behalf of the client in a probate matter. The invoice is in the name of the client.

Which of the following options best describes how the disbursement should be dealt with for accounting purposes?

A. A VAT-inclusive payment from the client account is recorded in the client ledger and cash sheet, providing there is sufficient client money available.

B. A VAT-exclusive payment is made from the client account, providing there are sufficient funds available for this purpose.

C. Ledger entries for a VAT-exclusive payment from the business account are recorded in the client ledger and cash sheet.

D. A VAT-exclusive payment will be made from the business account. The firm will recharge the client for the disbursement + VAT when it next bills them.

E. A VAT-inclusive payment is made from the business account. The firm will recharge the client for the disbursement + VAT when it next bills them.

QUESTION 3

A firm is instructed by the personal representatives of an estate in a probate matter. The acting solicitor instructs a house clearance company to clear the home of the deceased. The invoice is in the name of the firm and is for £800 + VAT.

What accounting entry is made in the client ledger when the firm pays the invoice?

A. Debit (DR) £960 client ledger client account.

B. DR £960 client ledger business account.

C. Credit (CR) £800 client ledger client account.

D. DR £800 client ledger business account.

E. CR £960 client ledger business account.

QUESTION 4

A firm acts for a client in two matters: the sale of her home, and the setting up of a trust for the benefit of her children. On completion of the house sale, there is a balance of £320,000 owed to the client. The client asks for £1,000 to be transferred to the trust matter on account of costs before the balance of the net proceeds from the sale of her home is sent to her.

What accounting entries are required to record this transfer?

A. Debit (DR) client ledger (sale) client account and credit (CR) cash sheet client account.

B. CR client ledger (sale) client account and DR cash sheet client account.

C. DR client ledger (sale) client account and CR client ledger (trust) client account.

D. CR client ledger (sale) client account and DR client ledger (trust) client account.

E. DR cash sheet client account and CR client ledger (trust) client account.

QUESTION 5

A firm has received a bank transfer from a client for £750 which has been paid into the client bank account. This sum represents payment of a bill for £550 (including VAT) which the firm sent to the client last week; and £200 towards future costs and disbursements.

Which of the following options best describes what the firm should do in this situation?

A. The firm should do nothing as the money is in the correct account.

B. The whole sum of £750 should be transferred promptly into the business bank account.

C. A sum of £550 should be transferred promptly into the business bank account.

D. The whole sum of £750 should be transferred promptly into the business bank account as it has been paid into the client bank account by mistake. A sum of £200 should then be transferred promptly back into the client account.

E. A sum of £200 should be transferred into the client bank account within two months.

■ ANSWERS TO QUESTIONS

Answers to 'What do you know already?' questions at the start of the chapter

1) Almost all law firms are VAT registered and must complete a VAT return every three months. They offset input tax that they have paid on supplies of goods or services to the firm against output tax that they have charged to clients on legal services supplied.

2) The correct answer was c) because the principal method is used when invoices are in the firm's name. Answer a) is wrong as there is no VAT charged on court fees and answer b) is wrong because it would be subject to the agency method of accounting for VAT as the invoice is in the name of the client.

3) Agency method:
   - DR client ledger client account (VAT-inclusive sum).
   - CR cash sheet client account (VAT-inclusive sum).

4) False. An *inter-client transfer* only involves how money within the client bank account is allocated. When money moves between the client and business bank accounts, it will involve *cash transfers*.

5) Inter-client transfer between two matters:
   - DR client ledger (matter A) client account.
   - CR client ledger (matter B) client account.

Answers to end-of-chapter SQE1-style questions

Question 1:

The correct answer was C. This is because each quarter, the firm must account to HMRC for output tax (VAT at 20% on £775,000 legal services supplied to clients = £155,000) less input tax (VAT at 20% on £175,000 paid to third parties for supplies of goods and services = £35,000). The amount owing to HMRC is therefore £120,000. Options A and B are wrong because the figures do not reflect the 20% VAT elements of the profit costs charged and invoices paid to suppliers (option B also has output and input the wrong way around). Option D is incorrect because it has input tax and output tax the wrong way around although the figures are correct. Option E is incorrect because it has both the figures and the input tax/output tax labels the wrong way around.

Question 2:

The correct answer was A. This is because the invoice is in the name of the client, so the agency method must be used. The payment can be made from the client account if there is a sufficient credit balance. Option C is wrong because the ledger entries should be for a *VAT-inclusive* figure using the agency method. Options B, D and E are all wrong because they more closely describe the principal method rather than the agency method. (Note that only option D correctly describes the principal method in any event.)

Question 3:

The correct answer was D. This is because as the *firm's name* is on the invoice, the firm must use the *principal method*. Therefore, a *VAT-exclusive* payment must be recorded as a debit on the client ledger, business account. Option A is wrong because it is VAT-inclusive and is paid from the client account. Option B is wrong because it is VAT-inclusive. Option C is wrong because it is a credit entry on the client account. Option E is wrong because it is a VAT-inclusive credit entry.

Question 4:

The correct answer was C. This is because an inter-client transfer must be made from the client's sale matter to her trust matter. There must be a DR entry on the client sale ledger (transfer out) and a CR entry on the client trust ledger (entry in), both in the client account columns. Options A, B and E are wrong because the cash ledger is not involved in an inter-client transfer. Option D is wrong because the debit and credit are the wrong way around.

Question 5:

The correct answer was C. The £750 payment is a mixed receipt of £550 business money (payment of a submitted bill) and £200 client money (on account of costs and disbursements where no bill has yet been submitted). As the bank transfer has already been paid into the client bank account, the business money element must be transferred into the business bank account promptly to comply with the Rules. Option A is wrong as business money cannot be kept in the client account. Options B and D are both wrong as the £200 client money element should not be paid into the business account. This would constitute a breach of the Rules. Option E is wrong because the client money element is already in the client account.

■ KEY RULES

The SRA Accounts Rules 2019 can be found on the SRA website.

The SQE1 Assessment Specification for Solicitors' Accounts does not require you to know individual Rule numbers, just the principles underpinning the Rules. However, you should familiarise yourself with the operation of:
• Rule 4.1
• Rule 4.2
• Rule 4.3
• Rule 6.1

7

Conveyancing accounts and other accounts

■ MAKE SURE YOU KNOW

This chapter is structured around elements of the SQE1 Assessment Specification relating to client money and client accounts in the context of conveyancing transactions, and the different types of accounts that solicitors and firms may deal with. It includes the following topics:

Accounting issues in conveyancing	Other accounts
Mortgage advances and redemptions	Joint account
• Mortgage advances	Client's own account
• Accounting entries – separate client ledgers • Accounting entries – single client ledger	Third-party managed accounts
• Mortgage redemptions	
Deposits	
• Stakeholder deposits	
• Accounting entries – separate stakeholder ledger • Accounting entries – seller's client ledger	
• Deposits held as agent	
Bridging loans	

■ SQE ASSESSMENT ADVICE

As you work through this chapter, remember to pay particular attention in your revision to:
• how law firms deal with mortgage advances using either the separate client ledgers method or the single client ledger method, including the associated ledger entries required for each method
• how law firms deal with mortgage redemptions

• how law firms deal with deposits held as either stakeholder or agent, including the associated ledger entries required for each method
• the different types of accounts, other than client accounts, which solicitors or firms may be associated with. These are joint accounts, clients' own accounts and third-party managed accounts.

■ WHAT DO YOU KNOW ALREADY?

Have a go at these questions before reading this chapter. If you find some difficult or if you cannot remember the answers, make a note to look more closely at that during your revision.

1) True or false? A solicitor can act for both a borrower and a lender in a conveyancing transaction.
   [Dealing with mortgage advances and redemptions, page 126]
2) What accounting entries would be used to record the receipt of a mortgage advance when using the single client ledger method?
   [Accounting entries – single client ledger, page 129]
3) What is a mortgage redemption?
   [Mortgage redemptions, page 131]
4) What is the difference between a deposit held as stakeholder and a deposit held as agent?
   [Holding deposits as stakeholder or agent, page 131]
5) What types of accounts, other than client accounts, may you be tested on in the SQE1 assessment?
   [Other accounts, page 136]

ACCOUNTING ISSUES IN CONVEYANCING

This section will focus on two accounting issues that are specific to conveyancing transactions (transactions involving the sale or purchase of property). It will consider the accounting requirements for:
• dealing with mortgage advances and redemptions; and
• holding deposits as stakeholder or agent.

It will also briefly consider bridging loans.

Dealing with mortgage advances and redemptions

Firms that offer conveyancing services may deal with **mortgage lenders** when acting for clients who are buying or selling properties. A buyer may need a **mortgage advance** to pay for the property that they are buying, and a seller may need to pay a **mortgage redemption** once their property is sold. For some transactions, a firm may act for both the borrower client and for the lender itself. In this context, the firm will have two clients. Both mortgage advances and mortgage redemptions will be considered in turn in the following sections.

Key term: mortgage lender

A mortgage lender is usually a bank or building society (although it can be a private lender) who lends money to a client to help them buy a property.

Key term: mortgage advance

A mortgage advance is the money that the lender has agreed to lend to the buyer so that they can complete the property purchase.

Key term: mortgage redemption

When a property is sold, the seller must repay the lender (or 'redeem') any money that is still owing on the mortgage. This repayment is called the mortgage redemption.

Mortgage advances

When a firm acts for both the lender and the buyer (who is borrowing the mortgage) in a property purchase transaction, the mortgage advance is usually held on behalf of the lender until **completion**. The firm should record the receipt of the mortgage advance in the ledgers by using either of the following two methods:

1) operate two separate client ledgers (one for the borrower and one for the lender) in accordance with Rule 8.1 of the SRA Accounts Rules ('the Rules' – see **Chapter 1**)

2) operate one client ledger, just for the borrower, but include the relevant details of the lender and any mortgage transactions in the details column of this ledger (the SRA have confirmed that this is acceptable practice although it falls outside a strict interpretation of Rule 8.1). Many firms use this method as it is simpler.

Key term: completion

The completion date in a conveyancing transaction is the date that the legal ownership of the property is transferred from the seller to the buyer. Although a deposit has usually been paid prior to completion, the remainder of the monies will be transferred to the seller on the completion date in exchange for the property.

When acting for both the lender and the borrower, a firm is entitled to charge both clients for the legal work involved. However, these charges are usually paid by the borrower.

1) If the firm has chosen to use separate ledgers for the lender and the borrower, it can record the profit costs and VAT for each in their

respective client ledgers (see **Chapter 5** for more information on submitting bills). However, the lender's charges can then be transferred to the borrower's client ledger to show that the borrower will be paying for both sets of charges.

2) If the firm is only using one client ledger (ie for the borrower), both sets of charges will be recorded on the same ledger, but as separate entries. The lender's charges must be clearly labelled as such in the details column.

Accounting entries – separate client ledgers

If the firm chooses to use two separate client ledgers, two sets of double entries are required to record the receipt of the mortgage advance:

1) to record the receipt of the mortgage advance in the lender's client ledger (*CR lender client ledger client account and DR cash ledger client account*); and

2) to transfer the mortgage advance from the lender's client ledger to the borrower's client ledger on the completion date (*DR lender client ledger client account and CR borrower client ledger client account*).

The firm will also need to make the following double entries when billing both clients:

1) To bill the buyer (borrower) for the legal work involved in the purchase (*DR buyer/borrower client ledger business account for profit costs and VAT; CR profit costs account and CR HMRC-VAT account*).

2) To bill the lender for the legal work involved in the mortgage (*DR lender client ledger business account for profit costs and VAT; CR profit costs account and CR HMRC-VAT account*).

3) To transfer the charges related to the mortgage from the lender to the buyer (*CR lender client ledger business account and DR buyer/borrower client ledger business account*).

These accounting entries are illustrated in the following case study.

Example ledger entries – separate client ledgers

A firm acts for Connor Green and Jack Jones who are buying a house together. They are borrowing £90,000 from MM Bank to help fund their purchase. This mortgage advance is received on 1st February. Connor and Jack have agreed to pay MM Bank's charges of £200 + VAT for the legal work associated with the mortgage. They will also pay their own charges of £500 + VAT for the legal work associated with the purchase. The firm bills both parties on 6th February, the completion date.

The ledger entries are shown in the separate client ledgers in **Figure 7.1** (for simplicity, the double entries in the cash sheet, and profit costs and VAT ledgers are not included). The entries relating to the different transactions are shaded differently for clarity.

| Accounting entries relating to the mortgage advance |
| Accounting entries relating to billing the clients |

Client ledger for the lender (extract)

Client ledger: MM Bank
Matter: Mortgage advance – Green and Jones

		Business account			Client account		
Date	Details	DR	CR	Bal	DR	CR	Bal
1 Feb	Cash – mortgage advance Green and Jones					90,000	90,000 CR
6 Feb	Green and Jones Purchase of 7 Guy Lane – transfer of mortgage advance				90,000		
6 Feb	Profit costs	200		200 DR			–
6 Feb	HMRC-VAT	40		240 DR			–
6 Feb	Green and Jones Purchase of 7 Guy Lane – transfer of profit costs and VAT		240	–			–

Client ledger for the buyer/borrower (extract)

Client ledger: Green and Jones
Matter: Purchase of 7 Guy Lane

		Business account			Client account		
Date	Details	DR	CR	Bal	DR	CR	Bal
	Balances carried forward			XX			XX
6 Feb	MM Bank – transfer of mortgage advance			XX		90,000	XX
6 Feb	Profit costs	500		XX			XX
6 Feb	HMRC-VAT	100		XX			XX
6 Feb	MM Bank – transfer of profit costs and VAT	240		XX			XX

Figure 7.1: Ledger entries to record a mortgage advance using the separate client ledgers method

Accounting entries – single client ledger

If a firm uses a single client ledger when acting for both the borrower and the lender in a purchase transaction involving a mortgage, all the accounting entries relating to both parties are recorded in the same buyer/borrower ledger. However, those relating to the lender must be clearly labelled as such in the details column.

The accounting entries to record a receipt of a mortgage advance using the single client ledger method is *CR buyer's client ledger client account and DR cash ledger client account* (ensuring that the *lender's name is included in the details column*, together with clear identification that the transaction relates to a mortgage advance).

Example ledger entries – single client ledger

The following case study is the same as that considered in the previous section (Green and Jones). However, here the ledger entries in **Figure 7.2** will illustrate how a mortgage advance, and charges for both borrower and lender, are recorded using the *single ledger method*. The entries relating to the different transactions are shaded differently for clarity. Italics are used in the details column to highlight the accounting entries that relate to the lender.

> Accounting entries relating to the mortgage advance
>
> Accounting entries relating to billing the clients

Client ledger for the buyer/borrower (extract)

Client ledger: Green and Jones Matter: Purchase of 7 Guy Lane							
		Business account			Client account		
Date	Details	DR	CR	Bal	DR	CR	Bal
	Balances carried forward			XX			XX
1 Feb	Cash – *MM Bank mortgage advance*			XX		90,000	XX
6 Feb	Profit costs	500		XX			XX
6 Feb	HMRC-VAT	100		XX			XX
6 Feb	Profit costs – *MM Bank mortgage advance*	200		XX			XX
6 Feb	HMRC-VAT – *MM Bank mortgage advance*	40		XX			XX

Figure 7.2: Ledger entries to record a mortgage advance using the single client ledger method

Practice example 7.1 illustrates how a question on this topic might be assessed in the SQE1 assessment.

Practice example 7.1

A solicitor acts for a client who is buying a new home, which she is financing by taking out a mortgage with an institutional lender. The solicitor also acts for the lender. It is the firm's policy to record mortgage advances in the buyer's client ledger rather than operating a separate ledger for the lender client.

What accounting entries are required to record the receipt of the mortgage advance?

> The accounting entries for the receipt of a mortgage advance using the single client ledger method are CR buyer's client ledger client account and DR cash sheet client account. The details column of the buyer's client ledger must include the lender's name and the identification of the monies as a 'mortgage advance'.

Mortgage redemptions

Sometimes firms act for both a lender and a borrower on a property sale transaction. In this situation they should operate two client ledgers, one for the lender and one for the seller/borrower, to record the accounting entries relating to the mortgage redemption.

The completion monies are *client money* so must be paid into the *client bank account*. When the completion monies are received, the firm can choose to either:

1) record the receipt of all the completion monies in the seller/borrower's client ledger and then transfer the mortgage redemption monies into the lender's client ledger by an inter-client transfer (see **Chapter 6** for more details on inter-client transfers); or

2) record the receipt of the mortgage redemption element direct in the lender's client ledger and the receipt of the remaining proceeds of sale in the seller/borrower's client ledger.

In either method, the mortgage redemption monies can then be repaid to the lender, and the net proceeds of sale (after deduction of the mortgage redemption monies and any other costs and disbursements) can be repaid to the seller (see **Chapters 5** and **6** for a fuller discussion of costs and disbursements).

Holding deposits as stakeholder or agent

When a firm acts for a client who is selling a property, it is usual for them to receive a deposit from the buyer's solicitors on **exchange of contracts**. Such a deposit can be held by the firm as either **stakeholder** or **agent**, depending on the terms of the contract. Each of these will be considered in turn.

Key term: exchange of contracts

When the solicitors representing the seller of a property have agreed the terms of the sale with the solicitors representing the buyer, both parties will sign their copy of the contract. The buyer pays a deposit (usually 10% of the purchase price) when the solicitors for the respective parties swap or 'exchange' the contracts. Exchange is the point at which the terms of the contract become legally binding. If the buyer wants to terminate the contract between exchange and completion, they are liable to lose their 10% deposit to the seller.

Key term: stakeholder

If a buyer's deposit is held by the seller's solicitor as *stakeholder*, it is held *jointly on behalf of both the buyer and the seller* during the period between exchange of contracts and completion. On completion, the deposit will belong to the seller.

Key term: agent

If a buyer's deposit is held by the seller's solicitor as *agent*, it is held *on behalf of the seller only*. This means that the deposit belongs to the seller from exchange of contracts rather than on completion.

Stakeholder deposits

Firms can use either of two methods when recording the receipt of a stakeholder deposit on exchange of contracts, as follows:

1) The firm can operate a *separate stakeholder ledger* in the names of *both the buyer and the seller*, in which the receipt of the stakeholder deposit can be recorded on exchange of contracts. On completion, the deposit can be transferred from the stakeholder ledger into the seller's client ledger.

2) The firm can record the receipt of the stakeholder deposit in the *seller's client ledger*. However, it must be *clearly labelled as stakeholder money*. This reflects the fact that the deposit does not belong to the seller until completion, and protects it from being inadvertently used to pay disbursements for the seller in the meantime.

Accounting entries for stakeholder deposits in a separate stakeholder ledger

If the firm chooses to use a separate stakeholder ledger, it will need to make the following accounting entries (journal entries):

1) Receipt of the stakeholder deposit on exchange of contracts – *CR stakeholder client ledger client account and DR cash sheet client account.*

2) Transfer of the stakeholder deposit on completion – *DR stakeholder client ledger client account and CR seller's client ledger client account.*

The following case study illustrates how these accounting entries would appear in the firm's ledgers.

Example ledger entries – stakeholder deposit in a separate stakeholder ledger

A solicitor acts for Bushra Ali who is selling her home. Exchange of contracts takes place on 1st October, at which time the solicitor receives a stakeholder deposit of £25,000 from the solicitors representing Lucy Stark, the buyer. It is the firm's policy to use separate stakeholder ledgers to record transactions relating to stakeholder deposits. Completion takes place on 9 October, at which time the deposit is transferred from the stakeholder ledger to Bushra's client ledger. The accounting entries for these transactions are illustrated in the ledgers in **Figure 7.3** and are shaded differently to reflect the different transactions.

| Accounting entries for receipt of stakeholder deposit |
| Accounting entries for transfer of deposit from joint stakeholder ledger to seller's client ledger |

Client ledger: Joint stakeholder ledger Bushra Ali and Lucy Stark (extract)
Matter: Sale of 8 Steep Hill

		Business account			Client account		
Date	Details	DR	CR	Bal	DR	CR	Bal
1 Oct	Cash – stakeholder deposit					25,000	25,000 CR
9 Oct	Bushra Ali – transfer of stakeholder deposit				25,000		–

Cash sheet (extract)

		Business account			Client account		
Date	Details	DR	CR	Bal	DR	CR	Bal
	Existing balances			XX			XX
1 Oct	Joint stakeholder ledger Ali and Stark – stakeholder deposit			XX	25,000		XX

Figure 7.3: Ledger entries for dealing with a stakeholder deposit in a separate stakeholder ledger

Client ledger: Bushra Ali (extract) Matter: Sale of 8 Steep Hill							
		Business account			Client account		
Date	Details	DR	CR	Bal	DR	CR	Bal
	Existing balances			XX			XX
9 Oct	Joint stakeholder ledger Ali and Stark – transfer of stakeholder deposit			XX		25,000	XX

Figure 7.3: (continued)

Accounting entries for stakeholder deposits in the seller's client ledger

If the firm chooses to record the receipt of the stakeholder deposit in the *seller's client ledger*, it must identify the deposit as stakeholder monies in the *details column* of the ledger.

The accounting entries (journal entries) to record this transaction would be the same as those required for any other receipt of client money – *CR client ledger client account and DR cash sheet client account.* However, the *details column* of the client ledger must clearly identify that the deposit is held as a *stakeholder deposit.*

Example ledger entries – stakeholder deposit held in the seller's client ledger

Using the case study from the previous section (Ali and Stark), the ledgers in **Figure 7.4** show the accounting entries required to record the receipt of the stakeholder deposit in Bushra Ali's client ledger. Italics have been used to highlight the information in the details column that identifies the deposit as stakeholder monies.

Deposits held as agent

If the contract terms provide for the buyer's deposit to be held by the seller's solicitors as agent for the seller, the deposit belongs to the seller from exchange of contracts. The receipt of the deposit will therefore be recorded directly into the seller's client ledger. Accordingly, the accounting entries are *CR seller's client ledger client account and DR cash sheet client account.*

Client ledger: Bushra Ali (extract) Matter: Sale of 8 Steep Hill							
		Business account			Client account		
Date	Details	DR	CR	Bal	DR	CR	Bal
	Balances carried forward			XX			XX
1 Oct	Cash – *stakeholder deposit held jointly for Ali and Stark*			XX		25,000	XX

Cash sheet (extract)							
		Business account			Client account		
Date	Details	DR	CR	Bal	DR	CR	Bal
	Balances carried forward			XX			XX
1 Oct	Bushra Ali – *stakeholder deposit held jointly for Ali and Stark*			XX	25,000		XX

Figure 7.4: Ledger entries for recording the receipt of a stakeholder deposit in the seller's client ledger

Practice example 7.2 illustrates how your understanding of this topic might be tested in an SQE1 assessment question.

Practice example 7.2

A solicitor acts for a client who is selling his house for £200,000. At exchange of contracts, the buyer's solicitors transfer the deposit of £20,000 to be held by the firm as agent.

What accounting entries are required to record the receipt of the deposit to be held as agent?

As the firm receives the deposit as agent for the seller, the deposit monies belong to the seller from exchange of contracts and can be

recorded as a receipt of *client money* in the seller's client ledger. The accounting entries will therefore be *CR £20,000 seller's client ledger client account and DR £20,000 cash sheet client account.*

Bridging loans

A bridging loan is money that a client may borrow, usually for a short time period, to 'bridge' a gap while they are waiting for other sources of money to become available. For example, in a conveyancing context, a client may use a bridging loan to buy a new property before selling their old property. In a probate context, the personal representatives administering a deceased's estate may use a bridging loan to pay the inheritance tax due on the estate while waiting for the deceased's assets to be sold.

The accounting entries (journal entries) required to record the receipt of a bridging loan are *CR client ledger client account and DR cash sheet client account.*

OTHER ACCOUNTS

As we have seen in **Chapters 1** and **2**, most firms operate general client accounts in which they hold client money. However, in this section, we will consider three other types of accounts that you need to understand for the SQE1 assessment. Such accounts hold money belonging to clients or third parties, and Part 3 of the Rules sets out the obligations on firms and solicitors when dealing with these other types of account:

1) Joint account (Rule 9).

2) Client's own account (Rule 10).

3) Third-party managed account (Rule 11).

As noted in **Chapter 1**, it is important to remember that the SRA requires firms and solicitors to act in the best interests of each client; and to safeguard money entrusted to them by clients and others (SRA Principle 7; Code of Conduct for Solicitors, RELS and RFLs Para 4.2; and Code of Conduct for Firms Para 5.2). These principles and regulations apply whether or not the money belonging to the clients, or third parties, is held in a firm's client account or in one of the three other types of account considered below. The SRA Principles and Codes of Conduct can be found on the SRA website.

Joint account

Sometimes an individual solicitor or a firm may be required to operate a joint account with a third party. One common example is if a client has named the firm or solicitor as an executor (a person or legal entity appointed by a person who has made a will to carry out the terms of their will) alongside another executor (or executors) who are not part of the firm, for example a family member or friend. Following the client's death, the executors can operate a joint account (rather than the firm's general client account) into which the money of the estate is paid. (See *Revise SQE: Wills and the Administration of Estates* for more details on the role of executors.)

Rule 9.1 provides that only two requirements from Part 2 of the Rules (client money and client accounts) apply to such joint accounts:

1) obtaining bank or building statements for the joint account at least every five weeks (Rule 8.2); and

2) keeping a central record of all bills or written notification of costs associated with the joint account (Rule 8.4).

See **Chapter 8** for more details on requirements for accounting records more generally.

Even though the other Rules in Part 2 do not apply, the solicitor or firm must still act in the client's best interest and safeguard their money by ensuring that any potential risks are minimised. For example, SRA guidance indicates that this may include requiring joint, rather than sole, signatures for withdrawals of money from the account.

Client's own account

Sometimes a solicitor operates a client's own bank or building society account on the client's behalf, for example where the client is unable to operate the account themselves due to a lack of mental capacity. In this situation, a solicitor may take on a specific role that allows them to operate a client's own account. A client who suspects that they will lose capacity in the future may appoint a solicitor as their *attorney* to manage their affairs under a **power of attorney**. Or a solicitor may be appointed as a **Court of Protection deputy** for a client who already lacks the mental capacity to manage their own affairs.

Key term: power of attorney

A power of attorney is a document by which one person can authorise another person to make key decisions on their behalf. The person who is given the authority is called the *donee* or the *attorney.* For example, a client may sign an *ordinary power of attorney* authorising a solicitor to sign documents and manage their finances for a temporary period while they are absent from the country. Alternatively, a client suffering from a debilitating or progressive illness may sign a *lasting power of attorney* for *property and financial affairs* to give a solicitor the authority to manage their affairs once they no longer wish to or are no longer capable of doing so themselves.

Key term: Court of Protection deputy

If a person does not have the mental capacity to make their own decisions, the Court of Protection may appoint a *deputy* to make decisions on their behalf and in their best interests. A solicitor may be appointed as a deputy, and as such, may be required to look after and make decisions involving money belonging to the person lacking capacity.

When a solicitor operates a client's own account as signatory, they can pay money in or out of the account. In addition to the solicitor's overriding obligations to act in the client's best interest and to safeguard their money, Rule 10.1 provides that three requirements from Part 2 of the Rules apply when operating a client's own account:

1) obtaining bank or building statements for the account at least every five weeks (Rule 8.2);

2) reconciling the statements at least every five weeks (Rule 8.3); and

3) keeping a central record of all bills or written notification of costs associated with the account (Rule 8.4).

The SRA recognises that it is not always possible to comply with Rules 8.2 and 8.3 when operating a client's own account. They have therefore issued guidance to clarify that providing the solicitor has taken reasonable steps to ensure that the client's money is not at risk, and to keep records of this, they will not be deemed to have breached the Rules.

Practice example 7.3 illustrates how this topic might be assessed in the SQE1 assessment.

Practice example 7.3

A solicitor has a client who has lost the mental capacity to look after his own finances following an accident in which he incurred serious head injuries. These injuries are permanent, so the Court of Protection has appointed the solicitor to act as deputy for the client.

What type of account should the solicitor operate to look after the client's money?

The solicitor should operate the client's own account as signatory in her role as court-appointed deputy. It is usual practice for a deputy to operate a separate deputyship account so that the money of the person lacking capacity is kept separate from money belonging to others. Therefore, it is not appropriate for the solicitor to hold the client's money in the firm's general client account.

Third-party managed accounts

Using joint accounts or operating a solicitor's own account is only appropriate when it meets the needs of an individual client.

However, **third-party managed accounts (TPMAs)** meet the needs of firms rather than individual clients. For example, some law firms choose not to operate their own client accounts and prefer to outsource the responsibility for looking after money belonging to clients and others to a third-party business which manages the money in *third-party managed accounts*. This is permitted under Rule 11.1, providing such law firms do not receive or hold clients' money themselves (Rule 11.1(a)). The SRA has issued specific guidance for firms who choose to use third-party managed accounts.

> ### Key term: third-party managed accounts (TPMAs)
> Some businesses offer account management services to law firms for a fee. This means that money belonging to clients or others is held in a bank or building society account that is managed and operated by the third-party business rather than the law firm itself.

Money belonging to clients or other third parties held in a TPMA does not fall under the definition of *'client money'* as it is not held by the law firm. Therefore, the firm does not have to comply with the stringent requirements of the Rules relating to *client money* and *client accounts*. Other advantages for firms of using a TPMA include:

- avoiding the costs associated with operating client accounts, for example, paying for professional indemnity insurance cover for risks to client money (insurance to protect firms from liability, for example, if a client loses money due to a solicitor's negligence in managing the client account) and instructing accountants to prepare reports (see **Chapter 8**); and
- reducing the risk of money laundering. (See *Revise SQE: The Legal System and Services of England and Wales* for more details on money laundering.)

However, firms must ensure that they only use TPMAs where it is in the best interests of their clients to do so, and where they are satisfied that the money belonging to clients or third parties will be safeguarded by the TPMA provider.

If using a TPMA, firms have certain obligations to both the SRA and to their clients. These include:

- checking that the TPMA provider is properly regulated by the Financial Conduct Authority (FCA);
- checking that the interest arrangements offered by the TPMA provider are appropriate;
- completing a TPMA notification form to send to the SRA as soon as the firm uses any TPMA – the form requires details of the TPMA provider, together with its authorisation number from the FCA;

- informing clients of the firm's arrangement with the TPMA provider and checking that clients understand any implications of this before accepting their instructions (Rule 11.1(b)). Firms should give a transparent and clear explanation of the terms of the firm's contract with the TPMA provider to their prospective clients, including specific information on how the TPMA fees are paid and who bears the cost (Rule 11.1(b)(i)). They should also tell the client of their right to terminate the agreement and dispute payment requests made by the firm (Rule 11.1(b)(ii)); and
- obtaining regular copies of statements from the TPMA to ensure that they accurately reflect any transactions (Rule 11.2). To do this effectively, firms should keep accurate internal records of any transactions to cross check against the TPMA statements.

Practice example 7.4 illustrates how your understanding of TPMAs might be tested in the SQE1 assessment.

Practice example 7.4

A law firm has chosen to outsource the responsibility for looking after money belonging to clients and others to a third-party managed account provider. Therefore, it does not operate its own general client account or any other client accounts.

What overriding obligations does the firm owe to its clients with respect to monies held in a third-party managed account?

The firm must ensure that it is acting in the best interests of its clients when using a third-party managed account provider. It must also ensure that the money belonging to clients or others is properly safeguarded while held in the third-party managed account.

Revision tip

Make sure you are familiar with the different requirements of Rules 9, 10 and 11 for solicitors operating joint accounts or a client's own account, or for firms using third-party managed accounts.

■ KEY POINT CHECKLIST

This chapter has covered the following key knowledge points. You can use these to structure your revision around, making sure to recall the key details for each point, as covered in this chapter.

- If a solicitor acts for both the borrower and the lender in a property purchase transaction, a receipt of a *mortgage advance* can be recorded using either the *separate client ledgers method* or the *single client ledger method*.

- If the *separate client ledger method* is used, the receipt of the mortgage advance will be recorded first in the lender's client ledger; then the mortgage advance will be transferred from the lender's client ledger to the borrower's client ledger using an inter-client transfer.
- If the *single client ledger method* is used, the receipt of the mortgage advance will be recorded in the borrower's client ledger, but the lender's details and identification of the transaction as a mortgage advance must be recorded in the details column of the ledger.
- If a solicitor acts for both the borrower and the lender in a property sale transaction, they must operate two client ledgers (for the borrower and the lender respectively) to record the *mortgage redemption*.
- A solicitor can hold a deposit as either a *stakeholder* (on behalf of both the buyer and the seller) or as *agent* (on behalf of the seller only) between exchange of contracts and completion.
- The receipt of a deposit held as stakeholder can be recorded using either the *separate stakeholder ledger method* (using a client ledger in the name of both buyer and seller) or the *seller's client ledger method* (identifying the deposit as stakeholder money in the details column).
- The receipt of a deposit held as *agent* should be recorded in the seller's client ledger as the money belongs to them.
- A solicitor or firm may be associated with accounts other than client accounts, such as a *joint account*, a *client's own account* or *third-party managed accounts*.
- When operating a *joint account*, a solicitor should obtain bank statements for the account at least every five weeks and keep a central record of all bills related to operating the account.
- When operating a *client's own account*, a solicitor should comply with the same requirements as for a joint account, in addition to reconciling the statements at least every five weeks.
- When using a *TPMA*, a firm should check that the TPMA provider is properly regulated by the FCA, ensure clients are informed properly about the use of the TPMA and their associated rights, and obtain and check TPMA bank statements regularly.

■ KEY TERMS AND CONCEPTS

■ SQE1-STYLE QUESTIONS

QUESTION 1

A client is buying her first house for £120,000. She is borrowing a mortgage of £100,000 from a building society to help finance her purchase. The solicitor acts for both the buyer and the lender with respect to this property purchase transaction. It is the firm's policy to use a single client ledger when acting for both the borrower and the lender.

What accounting entries should the firm use to record the receipt of the £100,000 mortgage advance from the building society?

A. Credit (CR) £100,000 buyer's client ledger client account and DR £100,000 cash sheet client account. The firm should include the building society's name and identify the monies as a mortgage advance in the details column of the ledger.

B. CR £100,000 building society's client ledger client account and DR £100,000 cash sheet client account. The firm should include the buyer's name and identify the monies as a mortgage advance in the details column of the building society's client ledger.

C. Debit (DR) £100,000 building society's client ledger client account and CR £100,000 buyer's client ledger client account.

D. DR £100,000 buyer's client ledger client account and CR £100,000 building society's client ledger client account.

E. There is no need for the firm to make any accounting entries as the mortgage advance must be paid direct to the seller's solicitors on completion rather than passing through the firm's accounts.

QUESTION 2

A client is selling his home for £350,000. When he purchased the house, he took out a building society mortgage for £200,000, of which £50,000 has yet to be repaid. The solicitor acts for both the seller and the building society with respect to this property sale.

How should the seller's solicitor record the receipt of the completion monies from the buyer's solicitor?

A. The seller's solicitor must record the receipt of all the completion monies in the seller's client ledger.

B. The seller's solicitor must record the receipt of all the completion monies in the seller's client ledger and then do an inter-client transfer to transfer the £50,000 mortgage redemption monies from the seller's client ledger to the lender's client ledger.

C. The seller's solicitor must split the completion monies and record the receipt of the £50,000 mortgage redemption monies in the lender's client ledger, and the receipt of any remaining proceeds of sale in the seller's client ledger.

D. The seller's solicitor can choose whether to record the receipt of all the completion monies in the seller's client ledger prior to transferring the £50,000 mortgage redemption monies into the lender's client ledger, or to split the completion monies on receipt so that the £50,000 mortgage redemption monies is paid into the lender's client ledger and the remainder is paid into the seller's client ledger.

E. The seller's solicitor can choose whether to record the receipt of the total completion monies into the lender's client ledger and then transfer the seller's monies into the seller's client ledger, or to record the receipt of the total completion monies into the seller's client ledger and then transfer the £50,000 mortgage redemption monies into the lender's client ledger.

QUESTION 3

A solicitor acts for a client who is selling their house for £350,000. On exchange of contracts, the buyer's solicitors transfer a deposit of £35,000, to be held as stakeholder. It is the firm's policy to use separate client ledgers when holding deposits as stakeholder.

What accounting entries should the firm use to record the receipt of the £35,000 deposit as stakeholder?

A. Debit (DR) £35,000 seller's client ledger client account and credit (CR) £35,000 cash sheet client account.

B. DR £35,000 stakeholder client ledger client account and CR £35,000 cash sheet client account.

C. CR £35,000 seller's client ledger client account and DR £35,000 cash sheet client account.

D. CR £35,000 stakeholder client ledger client account and DR £35,000 cash sheet client account.

E. DR £35,000 stakeholder client ledger client account and CR £35,000 seller's client ledger client account.

QUESTION 4

A solicitor is one of the joint executors named in a client's will, together with the client's son. When the client dies, both executors decide to set up a joint bank account to use while administering the deceased client's estate.

What obligations does the solicitor have while operating the joint account with the other executor?

A. The solicitor's only obligations are to act in the best interest of the joint executor and to safeguard any money and assets belonging to the deceased's estate.

B. The solicitor has no obligations with respect to money held in the joint account as it is not a 'client account'.

C. In addition to acting in the joint executor's best interest and safeguarding the deceased's estate, the solicitor should obtain account statements at least every five weeks.

D. In addition to acting in the joint executor's best interest and safeguarding the deceased's estate, the solicitor should obtain account statements at least every five weeks and keep a central record of bills or written notifications of costs.

E. In addition to acting in the joint executor's best interest and safeguarding the deceased's estate, the solicitor should obtain account statements at least every five weeks, reconcile the statements at least every five weeks, and keep a central record of bills or written notifications of costs.

QUESTION 5

A firm has decided to outsource its management of money belonging to clients and others to a provider of third-party managed accounts.

What information, if any, should the firm give to the Solicitors Regulation Authority (SRA) in connection with the firm's arrangement with the provider of the third-party managed accounts?

A. The firm must send the SRA a copy of their contractual arrangement with the third-party managed account provider.

B. The firm must notify the SRA that they are using a third-party managed account and send through details of the provider of the third-party managed account.

C. The firm must send copies of the statements of the third-party managed account to the SRA at least every five weeks.

D. The firm does not have to send any information to the SRA because money held in a third-party managed account is not client money.

E. The firm does not have to send any information to the SRA because the firm has no responsibility for clients' money that is held in a third-party managed account.

■ ANSWERS TO QUESTIONS

Answers to 'What do you know already?' questions at the start of the chapter

1) True. A solicitor may act for both a borrower and a lender in either a sale or a purchase transaction, for example, in a residential home conveyance.

2) CR buyer's client ledger client account and DR cash sheet client account. The details column must include the name of the lender and indicate that the transaction relates to a mortgage advance.

3) A mortgage redemption is the repayment by the borrower (the seller) to the mortgage lender of any money outstanding on the mortgage at completion.

4) A buyer's deposit held by the seller's solicitor as *stakeholder* is held jointly on behalf of both the buyer and the seller between exchange of contracts and completion. A deposit held as *agent* is held on behalf of the seller only until completion.

5) You may be tested on three types of accounts, other than client accounts, in the SQE1 assessment. They are *joint accounts, client's own accounts operated by a solicitor* and *third-party managed accounts*.

Answers to end-of-chapter SQE1-style questions

Question 1:

The correct answer was A. As the firm's policy is to use the single client ledger method when acting for both a borrower and a lender, it will only operate one client ledger for the buyer/borrower. The accounting entries will be in the client ledger as a credit entry in the client account, with a corresponding debit entry in the cash sheet client account. However, the details column must identify the receipt as a mortgage advance and name the building society so that it properly reflects the mortgage advance as being held on behalf of the lender until completion. Option B is wrong because if the firm's policy is to use a single client ledger in this context, the lender will not have a separate client ledger at all. Watch out for the exact wording used in the answers. Here options A and B are almost identical except for a couple of words (buyer rather than building society). Options C and D are both wrong because they describe inter-client transfers. Option C would be an appropriate answer if the firm used the separate ledger method instead, as it correctly describes an inter-client transfer from the lender to the borrower which might follow the receipt of a mortgage advance into the lender's ledger. Option E is wrong as there is no blanket requirement for mortgage advances to be paid direct from the lender to the seller's solicitors.

Question 2:

The correct answer was D. This is because the seller's solicitor can choose between the two methods described when receiving the completion monies. Option A is incorrect because it does not reflect the solicitor's duty to the lender in ensuring that the mortgage redemption monies are recorded in the lender's client ledger. Options B and C both describe legitimate ways for the solicitor to record the receipt of the completion monies, but the answers are incorrect because they both use the word 'must' rather than 'may' or 'can'. Option E is incorrect because it would be a breach of the Rules to record the seller's share of the completion monies in the lender's client ledger. Watch out for the terminology used in the SQE1 answer options. Some options may include words indicating compulsory actions, for example 'must'; some options may include words indicating preferred actions, for example 'should'; and some options may include words indicating legitimate choices, for example 'can' or 'may'.

Question 3:

The correct answer was D. This is because the firm's policy is to use separate client ledgers when holding deposits as stakeholder. The firm must therefore open a stakeholder client ledger in the joint names of both the seller and the buyer and record the receipt of the stakeholder deposit in this ledger. The deposit is client money and must be paid into the client account, so both entries will be in the client account columns. The credit entry is in the stakeholder client ledger and the debit entry is in the cash sheet. Option A is wrong because it refers to the seller's ledger rather than the stakeholder ledger, and the debit and credit entries are also the wrong way around. Option B is wrong because although it identifies the correct ledgers, the debit and credit entries are the wrong way around. Option C is wrong because it refers to the seller's ledger rather than the stakeholder ledger. Option E is wrong because it describes an inter-client transfer from the stakeholder to the seller's ledger. This would be appropriate to record the transfer of the deposit to the seller on completion.

Question 4:

The correct answer was D. This is because the solicitor has overriding responsibilities to act in the best interests of the client/the joint executor (under SRA Principles) and to safeguard money and assets belonging to clients (under the SRA Codes of Conduct). The solicitor also has obligations to obtain account statements at least every five weeks and keep a central record of bills or written notifications of costs (under the Rules). Option A is wrong as it only deals with the overriding obligations. Option B is wrong as the solicitor still has responsibilities for money held in a joint account. Option C is wrong as the solicitor's obligation to keep a central record of bills is missing. Option E is wrong as there is no requirement to reconcile statements for a client's money that is held in a joint account.

Question 5:

The correct answer was B. The SRA Guidance on 'Third-Party Managed Accounts' requires firms to complete and return a form which includes details of the third-party managed account provider. Option A is incorrect. Although the firm should notify *clients* of the key terms of their contractual arrangement with the third-party managed account provider (before accepting their instructions), there is no obligation to send a copy of the contract to the SRA. Option C is incorrect. Although the firm should obtain regular statements from the third-party managed account provider to ensure that they are accurate, there is no obligation to send copies to the SRA. Options D and E are both wrong because although the money held in the third-party managed account is not client money, the firm still has obligations to notify the SRA as outlined in option B. Option E is also wrong in that the firm still has responsibilities, for example, to act in the best interests of their clients and to ensure that their clients' money is safeguarded by the third-party managed account provider.

■ KEY RULES

The SRA Accounts Rules 2019 can be found on the SRA website.

The SQE1 Assessment Specification for Solicitors' Accounts does not require you to know individual Rule numbers, just the principles underpinning the Rules. However, you should familiarise yourself with the operation of:
• Rule 8.1
• Rule 8.2
• Rule 8.3
• Rule 8.4
• Rule 9.1
• Rule 10.1
• Rule 11.1
• Rule 11.2

Records, reconciliation and reports

■ MAKE SURE YOU KNOW

This chapter is structured around elements of the SQE1 Assessment Specification relating to the requirements relating to accounting records and accountants' reports. It includes the following topics:

> **Accounting records**
>
> • Internal accounting records
> • Statements and reconciliation

> **Accountants' reports**
>
> • Obtaining accountants' reports
> • Delivering accountants' reports
> • Other reporting obligations
> • Other requirements regarding accountants and accounting records

■ SQE ASSESSMENT ADVICE

As you work through this chapter, remember to pay particular attention in your revision to:
• the requirement to keep and maintain accurate records in client ledgers
• the different types of *accounting records* firms are required to keep
• the requirement to carry out *reconciliation* of the firm's ledgers against bank statements to double-check that their internal accounting records are accurate
• the general principle requiring firms to obtain *accountants' reports* after every accounting period
• the exceptions to this general principle
• the requirement to deliver accountants' reports to the SRA in some situations
• the requirements for storage and retention of accounting records.

■ WHAT DO YOU KNOW ALREADY?

Have a go at these questions before reading this chapter. If you find some difficult or can't remember the answers, make a note to look more closely at that during your revision.

1) What information must be included on a client ledger to ensure it is identifiable?
   [Accounting records, page 149]
2) Give three examples of different types of accounting records that a firm may hold.
   [Accounting records, page 149]
3) True or false? The process of bank reconciliation requires firms to cross-check the details of what is in the firm's client bank accounts against what is in the firm's business bank accounts.
   [Statements and reconciliation, page 152]
4) True or false? All accountants' reports must be delivered to the SRA.
   [Delivering accountants' reports, page 154]
5) How long must a firm retain and store its accounting records?
   [Other requirements relating to accountants and accounting records, page 156]

ACCOUNTING RECORDS

The main purpose of the SRA Accounts Rules (see **Chapter 1, The Rules, page 3**) is to keep client money safe. Many of the earlier chapters show how firms and solicitors deal with client money and keep it safe in the context of different types of financial transactions.

However, this chapter will focus on Rules 8, 12 and 13. These three Rules provide checks and balances so that firms can *prove* that they are complying with all the other Rules properly. They also provide regular opportunities for spotting any errors in the accounting records or risks to client money so that these can be resolved by the firm or, if the issues are sufficiently serious, reported to the SRA.

Internal accounting records

Rule 8.1 requires firms to keep accounting records that are *'accurate, contemporaneous* (ie kept up to date), and *chronological* (ie kept in the correct date order). The SRA has issued a supplementary guidance note, available from the SRA website, called 'Helping you keep accurate client accounting records', to give more details on how firms can comply with Rule 8.1. This guidance note recommends that firms use *double-entry book-keeping* principles (as demonstrated throughout this book).

Table 8.1 gives details of the types of internal accounting records that firms must keep.

Table 8.1: Different types of internal accounting records

Type of accounting record	Details	Rule number
Separate client ledgers for each client (and for each legal matter)	Firms must use separate client ledgers for each client (and matter). They must label each client ledger with the term *'client ledger'* and must include the client's name and a description of the legal matter (see **Chapter 2**)	Rule 8.1(a)
	Firms must record receipts and payments of client money on the client side of the ledger (ie in the client account columns) (see **Chapter 1**)	Rule 8.1(a)(i)
	Firms must record receipts and payments of business money, including bills for profit costs, on the business side of the ledger (ie in the business account columns) (see **Chapter 1**)	Rule 8.1(a)(ii)
Balances on client ledgers	Firms must keep a running total of all monies owed to clients (from adding up the balances on all the separate client ledgers)	Rule 8.1(b)
Cash sheet (cash book)	Firms must keep a cash sheet with a running total of all client account transactions (again, to show all monies owed to clients)	Rule 8.1(c)
Profit costs ledger	Firms must have a central record of all bills (or other written notification of costs) (see **Chapter 5, Submitting a bill**)	Rule 8.4
Transfers journal	Firms should have a separate record of all inter-ledger transfers (inter-client transfers) (see **Chapter 6, Inter-client transfers**). This record is often called the transfers journal	SRA Guidance Note

See **Figure 8.1** for an example of a client ledger relating to a very simple probate matter. It is annotated to give examples of some of these requirements for accounting records.

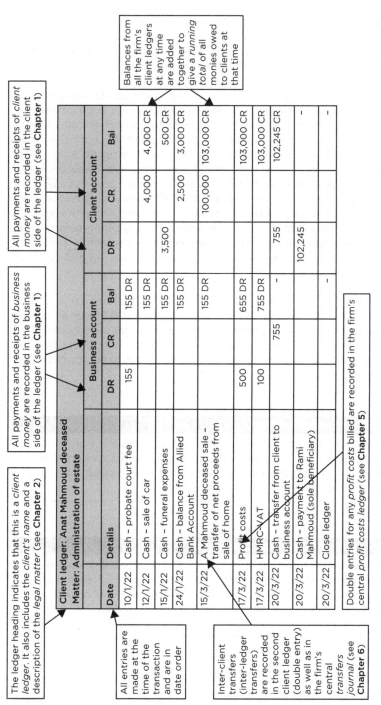

The ledger heading indicates that this is a *client ledger*. It also includes the *client's name* and a description of the *legal matter* (see **Chapter 2**)

All payments and receipts of *business money* are recorded in the business side of the ledger (see **Chapter 1**)

All payments and receipts of *client money* are recorded in the client side of the ledger (see **Chapter 1**)

Balances from all the firm's client ledgers at any time are added together to give a *running total* of all monies owed to clients at that time

All entries are made at the time of the transaction and are in date order

Inter-client transfers (inter-ledger transfers) are recorded in the second client ledger (double entry) as well as in the firm's central *transfers journal* (see **Chapter 6**)

Double entries for any *profit costs* billed are recorded in the firm's central *profit costs ledger* (see **Chapter 5**)

Client ledger: Anat Mahmoud deceased
Matter: Administration of estate

Date	Details	Business account			Client account		
		DR	CR	Bal	DR	CR	Bal
10/1/22	Cash – probate court fee	155		155 DR			
12/1/22	Cash – sale of car			155 DR		4,000	4,000 CR
15/1/22	Cash – funeral expenses			155 DR	3,500		500 CR
24/1/22	Cash – balance from Allied Bank Account			155 DR		2,500	3,000 CR
15/3/22	A Mahmoud deceased sale – transfer of net proceeds from sale of home			155 DR		100,000	103,000 CR
17/3/22	Profit costs	500		655 DR			103,000 CR
17/3/22	HMRC-VAT	100		755 DR			103,000 CR
20/3/22	Cash – transfer from client to business account		755	-	755		102,245 CR
20/3/22	Cash – payment to Rami Mahmoud (sole beneficiary)				102,245		-
20/3/22	Close ledger			-			-

Figure 8.1: Example client ledger with annotations

Statements and reconciliation

In the previous section we saw how *internal accounting records* such as client ledgers, the cash sheet (cash book), and other ledgers, for example the profit costs ledger, should be maintained to comply with the Rules.

However, firms are also required to obtain bank (or building society) statements for both their client accounts and business accounts at least every five weeks (Rule 8.2). This enables firms to cross-check their internal accounting records regularly against these statements for both client bank accounts and business bank accounts. This process of cross-checking is called **reconciliation** and must be undertaken at least every five weeks (Rule 8.3), although it can be done more frequently. *Reconciliation* provides a practical method for spotting any differences between the bank statements and the firm's ledgers. The focus of this reconciliation is on *client money* because the priority of the Rules is to keep client money safe. Any differences must be *investigated promptly* so that errors in either the firm's internal accounting records (or less often, the bank statements) can be resolved and corrected as soon as possible (Rule 8.3).

The **reconciliation statement** must be signed off either by the firm's Compliance Officer for Finance and Administration (COFA) or a manager of the firm (see key terms in **Chapter 3**) as evidence that the regular system of cross-checking has been completed and that any differences between the bank statements and the firm's internal accounting records have been identified and resolved promptly (Rule 8.3).

Key term: reconciliation

Reconciliation is the cross-checking system for comparing a firm's *internal* accounting records against its *external* bank statements. It must be undertaken at least every five weeks. Reconciliation ensures that any errors can be identified and resolved promptly.

Key term: reconciliation statement

The reconciliation statement (or reconciliation record) is a document recording confirmation that the reconciliation process has taken place. When the bank statements and the firm's internal accounting records match up, the COFA or a firm manager will sign the reconciliation statement (at least every five weeks) to confirm that all is in order.

Practice example 8.1 illustrates how requirements for accounting systems and controls in firms might be assessed in the SQE1 assessment.

Practice example 8.1

A firm obtains bank statements for its client and business bank accounts and conducts a reconciliation with its internal accounting records. This process highlights a discrepancy between them: the bank statements indicate that a total of £2,800,450 is held in the firm's client accounts at the bank, whereas the running totals from the firm's client ledgers and cash book indicate that the firm holds £2,800,500 of client monies.

What action should the firm take on discovering this discrepancy?

The firm should take prompt action to find out why there is a discrepancy of £50. The COFA cannot sign the bank reconciliation statement until it has been satisfactorily resolved.

ACCOUNTANTS' REPORTS

In the first part of this chapter, we looked at how firms are required to keep internal accounting records that are accurate, contemporaneous and chrono-logical. We also looked at how firms use the process of bank reconciliation to double-check that the internal accounting records are correct.

In this part of the chapter we will consider the additional requirements for an *independent accountant* to double-check the firm's accounting records. This provides an extra level of protection for *client money* because somebody *external* to the firm must look closely at the accounts to check whether all the Rules have been complied with.

Obtaining accountants' reports

Most law firms are required to employ an independent accountant to write a report at the end of every **accounting period**. The main purpose of the report is to identify whether the Rules have been complied with, and whether money belonging to clients or others has been placed at risk at any time during the period.

Key term: accounting period

A period (normally of twelve months) at the end of which financial statements are prepared in order to summarise the finances of the business for that period.

The general requirement under Rule 12.1(a) is that any firm that has held or received client money during the accounting period (including operating a joint account or a client's own account) must obtain an accountant's report within six months of the end of the period.

However, Rule 12.2 provides exceptions where there is perceived to be a lower risk to client money, either because the firm only receives client money from the Legal Aid Agency (Rule 12.2(a)) or because the firm only deals with small amounts of client money. If the balance on a firm's client account does not exceed an *average of £10,000* during the course of an accounting period, and also does not exceed a *maximum of £250,000* at any point in the same period, the firm is not required to obtain an accountant's report (Rule 12.2(b)).

Delivering accountants' reports

If the accountant discovers any breaches of the Rules when preparing their report for the firm, they must make a judgement as to whether the breach is sufficiently serious to justify **qualifying their report**. This would be the case where the breach means that client money has been, or is likely to be, placed at risk. If an accountant's report is qualified, the firm *must* send a copy of the report to the SRA within six months of the end of the accounting period (Rule 12.1(b)). There is no obligation on an accountant to qualify their report for less serious breaches of the Rules, and in such situations, there is no obligation on the firm to send a copy of the unqualified report to the SRA.

Key term: qualifying an accountant's report

If an accountant *qualifies* their report, it means that they have identified serious flaws in the firm's accounting records and/or systems and/or serious breaches of the Rules, such that client money has been, or is likely to be, put at risk over the accounting period. A *qualified accountant's report* is an important flag that something has gone wrong with the accounts.

However, the SRA has a right to ask firms to send copies of accountants' reports in situations where they consider that there may be a risk to client money, for example, where a firm closes down or stops holding client money. The SRA also has a broad right to request delivery of a report where it is 'in the public interest' (Rule 12.4). For example, if an employee of a firm has concerns about the safety of client money held by the firm, they may become a whistleblower and report their concerns to the SRA. In this situation it may well be in the public interest for the SRA to request a copy of the most recent accountant's report.

Practice example 8.2 illustrates how requirements relating to accountants' reports might be assessed in the SQE1 assessment.

Practice example 8.2

A firm's accountant has just prepared an accounting report for the firm's most recent accounting period. The senior partner notices that the accountant has qualified her report.

> What obligations does the firm have with respect to this report?
>
> **The firm must deliver a copy of the qualified accountant's report to the SRA within six months of the end of the accounting period to which it relates.**

Other reporting obligations on solicitors and accountants

In addition to the reporting obligations considered above, there are other legal and regulatory provisions that require firms, solicitors and accountants to report serious concerns more quickly to the SRA with respect to accounting practices and client money.

Under the SRA's Codes of Conduct for Firms and Solicitors, both firms and individual solicitors are under a duty to report *promptly* to the SRA any issues that may constitute a serious breach of the SRA's regulatory arrangements, including the Accounts Rules (SRA Code of Conduct for Firms Para 3.9 and SRA Code of Conduct for Solicitors, RELs and RFLs Para 7.7. Both Codes of Conduct are available on the SRA website).

An accountant must *immediately* report to the SRA any evidence of theft or fraud in relation to client money, or any concerns about whether a solicitor or firm is fit and proper to hold client money (s34 Solicitors Act 1974).

Practice example 8.3 illustrates how such reporting requirements might be assessed in the SQE1 assessment.

Practice example 8.3

A junior solicitor is checking the accounting entries on the client ledger for a complex and high-value probate matter in which she is assisting a more senior colleague. The junior solicitor has identified some suspicious withdrawals from the client account that are recorded on the client ledger. She believes that her senior colleague may have stolen substantial sums of money from the client account. The senior colleague (who is also the firm's COFA) is due to retire next week and is planning to move abroad imminently.

What action should the junior solicitor take?

As there is a serious and urgent risk to client money, the junior solicitor should report the matter to the SRA promptly. It may also be appropriate to report the matter to the police. It is not appropriate for the junior solicitor to wait until the firm's accountant prepares the accounting report as this may not be completed until six months after the end of the accounting period. This is likely to be too late to prevent further risks to client money.

Other requirements relating to accountants and accounting records

To be eligible for preparing and signing reports, accountants must be members of a chartered accountancy body (the Institute of Chartered Accountants in England and Wales (or 'of Scotland'); the Association of Chartered Certified Accountants; or Chartered Accountants Ireland) and must work for (or be) a registered auditor (Rule 12.5). However, the SRA may disqualify an accountant from preparing a report if they have been found guilty of professional misconduct by their professional body or if they have failed to exercise due care and skill while preparing a report (Rule 12.6).

Firms must provide all the information and documentation required by an accountant, including bank and other account details, so that they can prepare their report (Rule 12.8). The SRA also regulates the terms on which firms can engage accountants (Rule 12.7) and requires accountants to sign their reports in the prescribed form (Rule 12.9).

Firms are under an obligation to store all their accounting records securely for at least six years (Rule 13.1).

Revision tip

Remember the important time periods relating to accounting records and accountants' reports:

- Immediately – accountants must report *immediately* to the SRA any evidence of theft or fraud of client money, or concerns about fitness to hold client money.
- Promptly – firms and solicitors must report *promptly* to the SRA any serious breaches of the Accounts Rules.
- Five weeks – firms must obtain bank statements at least once every five weeks.
- Five weeks – firms must conduct a bank reconciliation at least once every five weeks.
- Six months – firms must obtain an accountant's report within six months of the end of the accounting period to which it relates.
- Six months – firms must deliver a *qualified* accountant's report to the SRA within six months of the end of the accounting period to which it relates.
- Twelve months – the normal length of a firm's accounting period.
- Six years – the length of time that a firm must retain and store securely all accounting records.

■ KEY POINT CHECKLIST

This chapter has covered the following key knowledge points. You can use these to structure your revision, making sure to recall the key details for each point, as covered in this chapter.

- Firms must keep *accurate, contemporaneous and chronological accounting records*, including client ledgers, a cash sheet, a profit costs ledger and a transfers journal.
- *Client ledgers* must be identifiable as such and should include the name of the client and the legal matter involved. Receipts and payments of client money or business money must be recorded in the client or business columns, respectively.
- Firms must *obtain bank statements* and conduct a *bank reconciliation* at least *once every five weeks*. The *reconciliation statement* must be signed off by a manager or the COFA of the firm once any differences have been investigated and resolved.
- Firms that hold, receive or are responsible for client money must obtain an *accountant's report* within six months of the end of the accounting period to which it relates. The primary purposes of the report are to *check compliance with the Rules* and to *identify any risks to client money*. There is no need to obtain a report if the client money held in the accounting period is only from the Legal Aid Agency, or if the amounts held fall below prescribed minimum thresholds.
- The accountant must sign the report in the prescribed format. If they identify any serious breaches of the Rules and/or risks to client money, they will qualify the report. A firm must deliver a *qualified accountant's report* to the SRA within six months of the end of the accounting period.
- Accountants must be members of recognised professional bodies but can be disqualified by the SRA from preparing reports for firms if they have been found guilty of professional misconduct or if the SRA finds that they have failed to exercise due care and attention in preparing reports.
- Firms must supply all details of bank accounts and internal accounting records to accountants so that they can prepare their reports.
- Firms must *retain and store accounting records* for six years.

■ KEY TERMS AND CONCEPTS

- reconciliation (**page 152**)
- reconciliation statement (**page 152**)
- accounting period (**page 153**)
- qualifying an accountant's report (**page 154**)

■ SQE1-STYLE QUESTIONS

QUESTION 1

A solicitor is about to take on the role of the firm's Compliance Officer for Finance and Administration (COFA). The solicitor wants to check that her firm is complying with the requirements for bank reconciliation.

What are the firm's obligations with respect to bank reconciliation?

A. The firm may obtain statements for all firm bank accounts every calendar month in order that they can be reconciled with the firm's profit costs ledger to identify and resolve any differences.

B. The firm should obtain bank statements for client accounts at least once per year in order that an annual accounting report can be produced by a qualified accountant.

C. The firm must obtain statements for all firm bank accounts at least every five weeks so that they can be reconciled with the firm's internal accounting records at least every five weeks, to identify and resolve any differences.

D. The firm must obtain bank statements for client accounts at the end of every calendar month in order that they can be reconciled with the firm's client ledgers and cash book to identify and resolve any differences.

E. The firm should obtain bank statements for all firm bank accounts every week in order that they can be reconciled with the firm's internal accounting records to identify and resolve any differences.

QUESTION 2

The Compliance Officer for Finance and Administration (COFA) has been asked to sign a bank reconciliation statement. However, on inspecting the reconciliation statement, the COFA identifies some differences between the firm's bank statements and the firm's internal accounting records.

Which of the following options best describes what action the COFA should take?

A. The COFA should sign the reconciliation statement and take no further action.

B. The COFA must report any discrepancies arising from the bank reconciliation to the Solicitors Regulation Authority (SRA) immediately.

C. The COFA should investigate and resolve any differences within six months, before signing the reconciliation statement.

D. The COFA should investigate any differences and then report any serious risks to client money to the SRA within twelve months.

E. The COFA should investigate and resolve any differences promptly, before signing the reconciliation statement.

QUESTION 3

An accountant has recently prepared the annual accounting report for a firm. The firm's partners note that the accountant has 'qualified' the report.

What action should the partners now take?

A. The report is qualified as it has been prepared by a qualified accountant. Therefore, there is no need for the partners or the accountant to do anything further.

B. The partners do not need to do anything as the accountant will send a copy of the report to the Solicitors Regulation Authority (SRA) immediately.

C. The partners must send a copy of the report to the SRA within six months of the end of the firm's accounting period.

D. The partners may instruct a different accountant to secure a second opinion as to whether the report should be qualified.

E. The partners must discuss the reasons for the qualified report with the accountant to identify and resolve any flaws in the firm's accounting practices.

QUESTION 4

A solicitor started up her own sole practitioner law firm eighteen months ago. She is primarily involved in criminal defence work, most of which is funded by the Legal Aid Agency. However, the solicitor has recently started to develop a private client department. The average balance of client money held by the firm during the most recent accounting period was £12,000, and the maximum balance at a point during this period was £50,000.

What are the firm's obligations with respect to obtaining an accountant's report for the most recent accounting period?

A. No accountant's report is required as most of the client money held by the firm in the accounting period is from the Legal Aid Agency.

B. The firm will need an accountant's report because it has held more than the prescribed minimum thresholds for client money in the accounting period.

C. No accountant's report is required because the client money held in the accounting period falls below the prescribed minimum thresholds.

D. The Solicitors Regulation Authority (SRA) requires all firms, including this one, to obtain, and then to deliver to the SRA, an accountant's report within six months of the end of the accounting period.

E. The SRA requires all firms, including this one, to obtain an accountant's report within six months of the end of the accounting period.

QUESTION 5

A solicitor clears out a storage cupboard in the former office of a senior partner who recently retired from the firm. In the cupboard, the solicitor finds some hard copy ledger books dating back five years. The solicitor is aware that the firm started using digital accounting software two years ago.

Which of the following best describes what the solicitor should do with the hard copy ledger books?

A. The solicitor should keep the ledger books safe for at least another year as accounting records must be retained and stored for six years.

B. The solicitor should keep the ledger books safe for at least another five years as accounting records must be retained and stored for ten years.

C. The solicitor should dispose of the ledger books as all accounting records must now be held in digital formats.

D. The solicitor should dispose of the ledger books as confidential waste immediately as they include sensitive financial information relating to clients.

E. The solicitor should dispose of the ledger books immediately as the firm may be liable for a fine from the Solicitors Regulation Authority for retaining accounting records for over three years.

■ ANSWERS TO QUESTIONS

Answers to 'What do you know already?' questions at the start of the chapter

1) A client ledger must be labelled as a *client ledger*. It must also include the name of the client and the details of the legal matter to which it relates.

2) Accounting records may include client ledgers, the profit costs ledger, the cash sheet (or cash book), the transfers journal and reconciliation statements.

3) False. Bank reconciliation requires firms to cross-check details of the firm's bank accounts against their internal accounting records such as their client ledgers. This process ensures that the internal accounting records are correct and enables any differences to be investigated and resolved promptly.

4) False. Only accountants' reports that have been qualified by a reporting accountant must be delivered to the SRA.

5) Accounting records must be retained and stored for at least six years.

Answers to end of chapter SQE1-style questions

Question 1:
    The correct answer was C. This is because firms must obtain bank statements for all firm bank accounts (both client and business accounts)

at least every five weeks. It also states correctly that the statements must be reconciled against internal accounting records (specifically the balances/running totals on the client ledgers and cash book) *at least every five weeks* to identify and resolve any discrepancies. The main purpose of bank reconciliation is to provide a regular check that the records are accurate with respect to how much client money the firm is holding. All the other options are wrong because they refer to incorrect time periods. Options A and B are also wrong because reconciliation is primarily focused on protecting client money rather than checking profit costs or preparing an accounting report. Watch out for the terminology used in the answer options. Some options may include words indicating compulsory actions, for example 'must'; some options may include words indicating preferred actions, for example 'should'; and some options may include words indicating legitimate choices, for example 'can' or 'may'. You must use your knowledge of the relevant Rules and principles to make a sensible choice.

Question 2:

The correct answer was E. This is because the COFA cannot sign the reconciliation statement until any differences have been identified and resolved promptly. Option A is incorrect as the COFA cannot sign the reconciliation statement while there are unresolved issues. Option C is incorrect as the Rules specify 'promptly' rather than within six months. Option B is incorrect as not all differences must be reported to the SRA, as many are minor and/or do not put client money at risk. These can be resolved straightforwardly. Option D is incorrect because if the COFA identifies any serious risks to client money, these should be reported to the SRA promptly rather than within a period of twelve months.

Question 3:

The correct answer was C. This is because an accountant will only *qualify* their report if they have identified serious breaches of the Rules, for example that client money has been or is at risk (option A is therefore incorrect). It is the firm's, rather than the accountant's, responsibility to send the qualified report to the SRA (so option B is incorrect) within six months of the end of the firm's accounting period. It is not appropriate to instruct a second accountant (option D), and although it may be sensible to discuss the report with the accountant in order to identify and resolve any flaws in the firm's accounting practices (option E), there is no requirement to do so in the Rules.

Question 4:

The correct answer was B. This is because although the maximum balance of client money in the accounting period is £50,000 (below the prescribed threshold), the average client money held in the accounting period is £12,000 (above the prescribed threshold). Therefore, the firm must obtain an accountant's report and cannot rely on the exemption. Option C is therefore wrong because the firm has held client money over the prescribed thresholds in the accounting period. Option A is incorrect because to rely on the exemption in the Rules, *all* rather than just *some* of the firm's client money must be received from the Legal Aid Agency in the period. Options D and E are incorrect because *all* firms are *not* required to obtain (and, in option D, deliver to the SRA) accountants' reports.

Question 5:

The correct answer was A. This is because, as there are no digital accounting records for the period covered by the ledger books, they must be retained and stored for at least six years in total (not 10 years or three years, so options B and E respectively are incorrect). Option C is incorrect as although most firms use digital accounting records, they are not obliged to do so. It will be sensible to dispose of the ledger books as confidential waste in due course, but they cannot be disposed of immediately (so option D is incorrect) and must be retained for at least another year.

■ KEY RULES

The SRA Accounts Rules 2019 can be found on the SRA website.

The SQE1 Assessment Specification for Solicitors' Accounts does not require you to know individual Rule numbers, just the principles underpinning the Rules. However, you should familiarise yourself with the operation of:

• Rule 8
• Rule 12
• Rule 13

Index